Building a Successful Archival Programme

CHANDOS
INFORMATION PROFESSIONAL SERIES

Series Editor: Ruth Rikowski
(email: Rikowskigr@aol.com)

Chandos' new series of books are aimed at the busy information professional. They have been specially commissioned to provide the reader with an authoritative view of current thinking. They are designed to provide easy-to-read and (most importantly) practical coverage of topics that are of interest to librarians and other information professionals. If you would like a full listing of current and forthcoming titles, please visit our web site **www.chandospublishing.com** or contact Hannah Grace-Williams on email info@chandospublishing.com or telephone number +44 (0) 1865 884447.

New authors: we are always pleased to receive ideas for new titles; if you would like to write a book for Chandos, please contact Dr Glyn Jones on email gjones@chandospublishing.com or telephone number +44 (0) 1865 884447.

Bulk orders: some organisations buy a number of copies of our books. If you are interested in doing this, we would be pleased to discuss a discount. Please contact Hannah Grace-Williams on email info@chandospublishing.com or telephone number +44 (0) 1865 884447.

Building a Successful Archival Programme

A practical approach

MARISOL RAMOS
AND
ALMA C. ORTEGA

Chandos Publishing
Oxford · England

Chandos Publishing (Oxford) Limited
Chandos House
5 & 6 Steadys Lane
Stanton Harcourt
Oxford OX29 5RL
UK
Tel: +44 (0) 1865 884447 Fax: +44 (0) 1865 884448
Email: info@chandospublishing.com
www.chandospublishing.com

First published in Great Britain in 2006

ISBN:
1 84334 162 X (paperback)
1 84334 175 1 (hardback)
978 1 84334 162 8 (paperback)
978 1 84334 175 8 (hardback)

© M. Ramos and A. C. Ortega, 2006

Typeset by Domex e-Data Pvt. Ltd.
Printed in the UK and USA.

Printed in the UK by 4edge Limited - www.4edge.co.uk

Contents

Appendices

Foreword

When I first heard that the authors were planning to write a book based on their own experiences in setting up an archival programme, I thought what a great addition this book could be to the literature already published on this subject. Now, the result of all their efforts is the personal and eminently readable guide you have in your hands. Without sacrificing clarity and without surrendering to jargon, this guidebook details just how to accomplish the overwhelming task of creating fully functioning archives out of the neglected contents of boxes stored away in closets and forgotten for years. This book is not a theoretical exercise. The authors base their advice upon the techniques and procedures that contributed to their success in creating an archival programme under less than ideal circumstances. I can only surmise that because no one advised them about the impracticable nature of their task, they proceeded on the assumption that their objectives were possible. Armed with enthusiasm, perseverance, and the protection afforded by a certain amount of naiveté, they were able to forge ahead and, in record time, create functional archives out of disarray.

The practical approach taken in this book in no way suggests that theoretical approaches to the subject are outmoded. Nor should you see this book as a justification for under-funding an archive or abandoning professional standards and ideals. On the contrary, it aims to be a systematic instruction manual that can place you on the path towards realising these ideals, complete with strategies on how to get the necessary funding and support. Unfortunately, organisations usually hire an archivist to begin an archival programme only after storing away a substantial backlog of material. Only then, when the parent institution becomes established enough to care about its past, and successful enough to require a way to access it, does the necessity of organising archives become a concern. The catalyst that leads to the creation of formal archives can come from many different sources: pressure by researchers for access to manuscripts, the need to document internal decision making, to launch an anniversary celebration or to promote itself to the world at large. The fact that the authors met these challenges makes this book a valuable resource, especially for newly hired archivists.

By sharing their experiences, the authors hope to share their success with you. They seek to offer practical assistance that will allow you to cope with the daunting task of establishing your archival programme. If find yourself in the position of a newly hired archivist dealing with the hitherto inaccessible records formerly in the care of an overworked clerical staff, then this book will set you in the right direction. Even if you are so fortunate as to be hired before they relegate the backlog of neglected records to the closet, this book will help ensure that you create a successful archival programme. It outlines a plan and sets a strategy so that in a relatively short amount of time, your parent institution will not know how it ever got along without you.

Diane Maher, University Archivist, Copley Library, University of San Diego

Preface

For the uninitiated, archives may seem mysterious. In actuality, however, archives are not much different from any other information centres, where access to information is paramount. I have been fascinated with archives for many years now, since I was an undergraduate at the University of Puerto Rico during the late 1980s. I used to spend hours of research at the General Archives of Puerto Rico, where I enjoyed long conversations with the archivists, as well as the quiet surroundings of the nineteenth-century hospital building where the archives are housed. I never thought that one day I would be part of this world.

As an archival student at UCLA, I realised that what I thought were complicated processes were really well-known, applied archival principles, theories and practices. Yet it was not until I had the opportunity to set up my first archives, that I realised that there was a lot more to establishing and running archives than I had imagined. I then had the opportunity to work with Alma Ortega. She had been hired as a librarian but was informed she was also in charge of the archives. Alma and I worked very diligently to establish an archival programme where none existed. We were able to combine our expertise in these two closely related disciplines, library and archival sciences. The result of this collaboration was the basis of this book.

Having gone through the process of starting an archival programme from the ground up, we had at one point considered writing up the whole process to help others faced with the same challenges. When the prospect of writing such a book came two years later, we genuinely welcomed the opportunity to tell others about our experience, knowing that this work added a different perspective to the existing literature on setting up an archival programme.

Our goal was to write a very practical book for individuals with little to no experience in archives – individuals who are suddenly entrusted with taking care of the archives at their institution. We wanted to help jumpstart this process – but with direction. We wanted to tell you not to panic! We have been there and were able to accomplish it! We wanted our book to be encouraging and as uncomplicated as possible, but more importantly, we wanted to emphasise to anyone confronted with the task of starting an archival programme from scratch that it is indeed possible.

We hope that we have achieved this goal. After reading and applying what is in this book, you will have a functional archive. An archive that you can eventually build upon as you learn more about archives and their management.

Marisol Ramos and Alma C. Ortega, San Diego, CA

About the authors

Marisol Ramos has been involved in archives and libraries for many years. She received a BA in Anthropology at the University of Puerto Rico, Río Piedras. As an anthropology student, she became interested in ethno-historical research. This interest took her to the State University of New York-Albany, where she pursued a graduate degree in Latin American and Caribbean Studies. As part of her research, she travelled to Puerto Rico to study nineteenth-century water rights in Southern Puerto Rico, where she had access to the archival collections at the Archivo General de Puerto Rico. In 1996, after earning her master's degree in Latin American and Caribbean Studies, Marisol moved to Southern California seeking professional research opportunities.

Dissatisfied with the different research positions she held during her first few years in Los Angeles, Marisol decided to pursue a career path in archival sciences. In 1999, she was accepted into the master's programme at the Department of Library and Information Studies at the University of California, Los Angeles (UCLA). From 2000 to 2002, as a student and after graduation, she worked as an archival processor at UCLA's shared processing facility. During this period, she became conversant with a wide variety of archival materials, such as manuscripts, books, photo albums, VHS tapes, prints, and the like. She processed several collections such as the *Edgar Bowers Papers* and *The*

Hunger Strike for Chicano Studies at UCLA, while also assisting in processing large collections such as the *June Wayne Papers, Collection of Eighteenth, Nineteenth and Early Twentieth Century Political Cartoons* and *From the Earth to the Moon, Collection of Research Materials for the HBO Television Series.*

In January 2003, Marisol was hired as the first archivist at the Chicano Studies Research Center Library at UCLA where she established an archival programme. Currently, she is working as a research librarian at the Virginia Reid Moore Marine Research Library at the Cabrillo Marine Aquarium in San Pedro, California. Marisol resides in southern California.

Alma C. Ortega is an assistant professor for Copley Library at the University of San Diego, California. She is a reference librarian and bibliographer for the areas of history, Spanish language and literatures, and ethnic studies. She also teaches course-integrated sessions, works with archival collections and conducts research on collection management, the place of archives in libraries, and Romance languages. She earned two bachelor's degrees in Peace and Conflict Studies and in Spanish (Iberian Languages and Literatures) from the University of California at Berkeley (1996) and two master's degrees in Library and Information Studies (2002) and Latin American Studies (2003) from the University of California, Los Angeles (UCLA). She has been working in libraries since 1998.

Alma developed an interest in archives and rare books while in library school and used primary resources extensively in historical geography research. From 2002 to 2003, Alma was the library director at the UCLA Chicano Studies Research Center Library. In that position, she pressed for the hiring of the first archivist to help assess the 30+ year backlog of collections. Under her direction, an archival programme was set up at the centre in six short months. She has professional work experience in a variety of library settings ranging from public, academic, special, law, and research libraries. All of the libraries in which she has worked to date possess archives. She resides in San Diego, California.

The authors may be contacted at the following:

E-mail: *marisol@palantech.com* and *alma@sandiego.edu*

Introduction

The purpose of this book is to provide best practices and solutions on how to establish successfully an archival programme through a practical approach, without using too much technical or theoretical jargon. Conversely, this book may serve as a companion text to a theoretical archival course. It will provide easy-to-follow advice and set achievable goals for starting an archival programme in an environment where a small budget or even 'no budget' can threaten the future of the archives.

Why this book?

We felt that a book that offered basic and concise advice was needed by anyone who was suddenly given the task of setting up a new archival programme in a short period of time. If you have ever looked for the steps to setting up an archival programme, you may well have only found dense materials that are too theoretical and offer very little practical advice. The hope here is to demystify and facilitate the process.

I was working as a librarian when I was told that my responsibilities included managing the 300+ boxes that were called 'the archives'. Having not been trained as an archivist, I had the opportunity to go through the very journey you are about to embark upon, or perhaps find yourself already in the middle of, without knowing what to do next.

It is difficult to know where to get started. I kept asking different people and getting different answers. The books and materials I came across were too dense and I simply did not have the time to become an archivist while still managing all my other duties, primarily running the library. This is when Marisol Ramos, a trained archivist, came in. As an archivist and fellow UCLA library school alumna, I asked her to help me put the archives in order. That was the beginning of our long-standing collaboration. We toiled together and created our own method of organising the archives on a minimal budget and resources. We kept on tweaking along the way and, honestly, one day it *was* all under control.

As already mentioned, you will find very little jargon in this book, and when it *is* used, the layman's term will also be given or you can refer to the glossary at the end of the book. We hope that by following the paths of action described in each chapter, this book will help you to set up your archives. For many aspects, minimum specifications are provided. However, even where you are unable to meet these specifications, you will, at least, know what you need to aspire to, so that you can eventually build your own successful archival programme.

Let us get back to our experience. At the end of six months, in addition to having dealt with the 300+ boxes, here is a list of what we accomplished:

- an inventory survey was performed and box inventory lists were identified as such, instead of being called 'finding aids';
- we developed a mission, a vision and goals and objectives;

- we created an assessment tool;

- acquisitions/donation and deaccession policies were established;

- a collection file was created for each collection;

- a donors' registry was set in place;

- finding aid templates were created to facilitate processing;

- a processing room, with adequate storage space, was set up.

We were able to transfer the materials from all the acidic boxes into acid-free boxes and, when possible, acid-free folders as well. Budget is extremely important, but in case you cannot afford the complete transfer of your materials into an acid-free environment, we will let you know what you can do to protect your archival materials in the meantime.

The entire process, from beginning to end, was done in an amazing six months. I say 'amazing' because we each still had other major responsibilities going on at the same time. A lot of work went into this project, but through our experience we want to assure you that it *can* be done, all you have to do is tackle it one piece at a time. To make the process less daunting we have created samples and templates for you to use and record your progress in all of the major areas needed to establish a successful archival programme.

In this book we rarely discuss archival theory or the history of archives or the archival profession. This is a deliberate decision. Our focus is a practical one, where we jump straight to getting the job done. This approach does not in any way discount the value of archival theory or the historical background of the archival profession; on the contrary, we are applying archival theory directly through action. We hope that as you learn to do your job and establish your archives, you become interested in learning more about this wonderful profession. For those of you who are eager to expand your knowledge of the theoretical underpinnings of archives, a further reading section is provided at the end of the book.

I was very lucky to end up with two of us working on this project, otherwise it just would have taken longer than six months. With the blueprint found in this book, the clean-up and set-up process still would have been achieved within a year. One year to set up an archival programme single-handedly is an incredible feat, not to mention a very good timeframe indeed!

So here again is what we hope you will get out of this book:

- easy paths of action;

- practical approaches;

- advice on how to build relationships between the archives and the donors (after all, without them, there would be no archives!)

Challenges facing archives

Archives today face many challenges; from the basic acknowledgment of the important functions they play within the parent institution, to receiving the funding necessary to maintain functioning archives. More often than not, archival departments are underfunded and underappreciated. When budget cuts are applied to an institution, archival departments tend to be the hardest hit. There are many reasons why this is so and here are four salient ones:

- *Social invisibility*: Archives are usually located in hard-to-access, out-of-sight places (basements, attics, in the backs of buildings). People are vaguely aware of their existence, but this is not knowledge that sticks in their minds.

- *Misunderstanding of the purpose of archives*: To laypeople (your supervisors, co-workers in other departments, donors and the general public) archives are just big rooms full of *stuff*. A place to store *important stuff* that someday, someone will want to see.

- *Space usage*: Archives, just like libraries and other information centres, need a lot of space, physical or virtual. Even the new generations of electronic media (magnetic tapes, CDs, DVDs and web servers) take up a lot of space. And space is a scarce commodity that costs money to acquire and maintain.

- *Cost*: Finally, the operation of properly-run archives is extremely expensive. You need acid-free boxes and folders, a lot of shelve storage for the collections' boxes, a controlled environment (not too hot and not too humid) and most importantly, people. These people are the processors, archivists, curators, conservators; and they all need salaries. When budgets are allotted, archives do not and may not have any control of how much money they will get to keep running.

Yet archives are created because they are needed. Sometimes they begin with the generous contributions and strong influence of a donor. The institution or centre receives a gift, so space is needed to store the collection and someone needs to be hired to make the collection accessible through exhibitions, websites, displays, etc. to fulfil the donor's wishes. If you are lucky, monies are allotted in the budget to set up the archives. Occasionally, though, an archival programme just happens. Slowly but steadily, boxes are brought in, stored somewhere and quickly forgotten until, 20 or 30 years later, someone cries: We have an archive! It is at this point that you may have been hired or volunteered to take control of the *archives*.

If you are fortunate, you have an archival degree or, lacking that, some knowledge about how archives are run. Most often, however, this is not the case. The goal of this book is to get people who do not know much about archives to understand what they entail, so that they learn not only how to set up a programme, but also how to organise it and market it to their parent institution in order to survive and gain it a more respectable place within the parent institution.

Justifications for archiving the right way

Regardless of how you got your position, you want to do a good job. We know why you want to do it right. You have been entrusted to protect, preserve and make information accessible for future generations. You are hopeful that the archives will be available for decades and centuries to come. What seem like obvious reasons to you are not necessarily that clear to your supervisors. So you need to sell your job and your archives. It may sound sacrilegious to view our work as akin to that of businesspeople running a company, but that is exactly the way we want you to see yourself.

In the current global financial environment, information centres of any kind – be they libraries, archives or cultural/community centres – need to become more competitive in order to retain the minimum funding needed to continue their work. On behalf of your stakeholders, those individuals who have a 'stake' on the materials that you are preserving in the archives, you need to market the need to create and keep the archives functional for years to come. These stakeholders are your supervisors, their superiors, boards of directors, town mayors, university deans, donors, co-workers, community leaders and on and on. Your job is to make all the stakeholders aware of the many ways in which supporting the archives is a good investment. Some cases in point:

- *Senior management/administrators/directors*: You can identify ways to use archival collections to highlight new sources of revenue for the parent institution. For example, Coca-Cola® researches its archives to design new commercial campaigns using materials from past campaigns, such as photographs, scripts, storyboards, etc.

- *Boards of directors*: Show them how the money you are receiving from them is helping achieve the mission of the institution. For example, use your annual report to showcase how you use the supplies you have bought to preserve the collections.

- *Donors*: Whether individuals or organisations, etc., donors need to see what you have done with their donations. For example, exhibitions (traditional or virtual), commemorative events, books created using materials from the collection.

- *Communities/minorities/groups represented in your collection*: Reach out to your surrounding communities and other groups represented in your collections. Show them how the archives are relevant to them. Offer them tours to the archives and display collections that speak to them.

The main idea is to advertise how the archives matter to all of your stakeholders. The keyword is to be *proactive*. You will read it many times throughout this book. You have to forget the image of archives as old buildings with 'stuff' and reinvent the role of the archives as a living entity that is pertinent to this modern age. Archives are actually the bridges between the old and the new, and both are worth preserving for future generations.

Organisation of this book

This book is a collaborative work. We are both information specialists, but with different specialisations: archives and libraries. Throughout the book we use *I* or *we*, depending on who is the main voice. Chapters 3, 4, 5 and 7 were written by the archivist, as well as the sections on needs assessment in Chapter 2 and preservation in Chapter 6. The librarian wrote the sections regarding strategic planning and evaluating the financial requirements for a thriving archival programme on a budget in Chapter 2, workspace scenarios and setting up the physical space in Chapter 6 and the sections on citing archival materials in Chapter 8. Chapters 1, 8 and 9 were written jointly. The language in this book is very informal and colloquial. This is knowingly done, as we want to engage you positively into this project of establishing your archives. We want you to benefit from this process and realise that, although a daunting enterprise, it can be done. We went through it and survived and so will you!

Unless noted otherwise, the word *archives* is used to signify the archival programme and the words *archive* and *repository* are used when referring to the physical building where archival collections are housed.

First steps

Needs assessment: the tool to start creating your archives

Finding the right tool to emphasise the needs of any archives is vital in these times of tight budgets and limited resources. One such tool is a needs assessment study. This is a document that highlights the advantages of either creating or continuing to support an archival programme. Problems can be discovered and a plan of action with specific recommendations and goals can be set forth to guide the future development of your archives. Needs assessment studies serve to inform the process of creating the mission, goals and objectives for your programme, which will help you generate the strategic plan and the necessary archival policies to guide the management of a thriving archival programme. Moreover, needs assessment studies are useful instruments when applying for grants and other types of governmental or private funding. Most of the information gathered to create a needs assessment study is also required when writing grant proposals. This all-in-one document is a major key to success. Do not skip this first step.

Components for the creation of a needs assessment study

Needs assessment studies are not difficult documents to write up but they *can* take time depending on the size and resources of the programme to be assessed. Ideally, an archival background would help you to identify better the specific needs of your collection, but we know that is not a possibility at the moment. This document provides you with the opportunity to set the right course for your programme, while drawing the attention of administrators and donors to your needs and giving them the necessary reasons to want to devote precious resources to setting up an archival programme. The list of components can be simplified or expanded as necessary.

After writing your first needs assessment study, you will find that you have gained a better sense of the task at hand: how hard, how long and how difficult it will be to start your archival programme. Do not be afraid if the task seems overwhelming. Any beginning seems that way, but we know from experience that it can be done.

The steps for a needs assessment study are detailed below. Panel 2.1 provides some definitions on research methodologies for your needs assessment study.

Introduction

Explain the history of your institution and why this report is important for the archives. Identify whom the archives will serve and how their current condition positively or negatively affects current and future users. Explain what kind of assessment you want to do. For example, an archival assessment evaluates the collection's needs, its policies and procedures, while a facility assessment appraises the physical conditions where the archives will be housed.

Methodology

Explain how you gathered your data. If you used quantitative or qualitative methodologies or a combination

Panel 2.1: Definitions on research methodologies for your needs assessment study

Quantitative methods: Numerical tabulations and statistical comparisons made possible by systematic surveys, observations, or analysis of records. Data are used to test hypotheses and identify the strength of patterns observed using qualitative methods.[1]

Qualitative methods: Ways of collecting information on the knowledge, attitudes, beliefs and behaviours of the target population.[2]

Mixed methods: This is a type of research in which both qualitative and quantitative approaches are used in types of questions, research methods, data collection and analysis procedures and/or inferences.[3]

Survey: A method of collecting information directly from people about ideas, feelings, etc. A survey can be a self-administered questionnaire that someone fills out alone or it can be completed with assistance. A survey can also be an interview that is done in person or by phone.[4]

Questionnaire: A group of written questions to which subjects respond. Some restrict the use of the term 'questionnaire' to written responses.[5]

of both to assess the archives' needs, give a clear explanation of how, when and what kind of information you collected. To gather the best data, use a combination of quantitative (inventories, questionnaires, surveys) and qualitative methods (focus groups, one-on-one open-ended interviews) to achieve a better understanding of your organisation, your available resources, the needs of your constituents and the archival programme itself. Check the appendices for inventories and questionnaire templates to help you get started in your data gathering. In the following sections, you will use the information gathered to classify, summarise and highlight the specific needs of your archives. (See Appendix A for a collection survey template and Appendix B for an inventory worksheet template).

Identify all the factors impacting the collection

- *Physical condition*: Make a list of the condition of your collection, e.g. water damage, brittleness and pest damage. When assessing the physical condition of the collection, ask the following questions:
  - What is the condition of materials? For example, brittleness, water damage.
  - Where is it located? For example, warehouse, attic, basement.
  - Is it housed properly? For example, acid-free boxes, acidic boxes, biscuit/cookie tin.
  - Is it infected with pests or mould? For example, cockroaches, silverfish, mould.
- *Preservation/conservation issues*: After assessing the physical condition of the collection, you should then list what preservation/conservation projects are most critical for the archives. For example, making preservation copies using acid-free paper can preserve scrapbooks and newspaper clippings collections that have become yellowed or brittle. Do not forget electronic media (diskettes, CD-ROMs, audio tapes). Ask yourself the following questions:
  - Can the information still be read?
  - If the information is lost, is there a substitute available?

- Do you need to migrate your current technology to new formats?
- How much would it cost to save these materials?

List the problems that you find and provide possible solutions and possible cost.

- *Uniqueness of the collection*:
  - Explain how your collection is unique.
  - What makes it special?
  - How does it differ from other institutions' collections?
  - Why is it worth the time and money to preserve?
- *Ownership/copyright issues*:
  - Does your institution have ownership of the collections?
  - Do you keep records for each collection in the archives?
  - Do you have the right documentation, such as deeds of gift, current donors' contact information?
  - Who owns the copyrights of your materials – you or the donor?
- *Clientele*:
  - Identify your users.
  - Use questionnaires, phone surveys and focus groups to find them, as they are not only your users but also potential donors.

Summary of results

- *Types of records*: List the types of records in your collection:
  - print (books, correspondence, journals);
  - media (CD-ROMs, DVDs, diskettes);
  - memorabilia (diplomas, trophies, medals).

- *Quality of collections*:
  - Do you need to deaccession?
  - Will the collections stand the passage of time?
  - Single vs. multiple copies.
  - Reliability: Can you trust the information?
- *Opportunities for growth*:
  - List any areas in the collection that should be expanded and why.
  - In what other areas should the archives be collecting?

Cost estimate to start/maintain the collection/archives

At this point only estimate the cost of supplies and personnel required for the job. Include, for example, an archivist (you), your assistant, a manuscript processor, etc.

Conclusions and/or recommendations

Recap the purpose of the report, the most important or significant findings and your recommendations to resolve these problems.

The strategic plan and your organisation's needs

This section could have been more in-depth, but as the focus of this book is building a successful archival programme through a practical approach, we feel that there are plenty of books and websites already in existence that can help you further develop these areas of your strategic plan. The aim of this section is to acquaint you at the basic level with how to create a mission, vision, goals and objectives and the skeleton of the strategic plan without getting into deep philosophical discussions about value statements or any other such matters. As already mentioned, we know that there already exist many great books on this topic, but we are not here to reinvent the wheel; we are here to get it rolling! And at a good speed, might we add, so you can start functioning and, in due course, be able to revisit your progress. In the meantime, however, be assured that following these steps will get you there and that you will have fulfilled all of the requisites.

It is always good to start any venture with a plan. While you are doing that, why not also develop a plan for the future? The sooner you think about the future, the fewer surprises there will be in the long run. Although it may seem obvious, it does take some time to get organised. So as you move forward with your thoughts about the eventual place of the archives, do not doubt that these future plans will be achieved. A strategic plan is meant to create some work, but mostly future work. In the early stages, you are merely projecting where the archives will be one day.

The action plan

To begin, you need a plan of action. This is made up from a number of significant pieces, namely, the mission, the vision and the goals and objectives. These are essential to creating a successful archival programme, not just the strategic plan for the archives. Spending a good amount of quality time on creating these parts is very important. You really do not want to find yourself writing all of these elements while you are creating the strategic plan. You could, but the point of this plan is to make the process as easy as possible. Keep in mind, however, that your quality input will still be required. If you want to do this once and right, skimping is not an option.

To recap, it is strongly recommended that you create the archives' mission, vision and goals and objectives, in that order *before writing the strategic plan*. This will help the process go much more smoothly. So let us begin with the mission statement. How do you write a mission statement? What does it entail?

The mission statement

The mission of the archives should be simple, concise and short. It should: (1) be about the organisation; (2) tell what it does; and (3) mention for whom the archives were created and whom they aim to serve. Mission statements are usually reviewed every three to five years. In developing your mission statement, it may help to see the mission as a 'statement of purpose' for the archives. Ask yourself: why do the archives exist? (See Appendix C for samples of mission statements).

The vision statement

Currently, there are two definitions in use for a vision statement. The first and more traditional definition sees the vision statement as a description of the state and function of the organisation. More recently, a second definition has emerged in which the vision statement is seen as a statement that challenges and inspires an organisation to achieve its mission. The vision can be short or long, depending on how and where you see the archives at present and in the future.

A vision can be a single statement or a list of actions to be taken to fulfil the mission. It can also be a statement that inspires you to achieve your mission. Visions tend to get revisited about once a year and the things that have been improved upon are replaced by new challenges.[6] (See Appendix D for samples of vision statements).

Goals and objectives

Simply put, goals are desired outcomes. Goals are made up of objectives, and objectives are the actions that achieve the goal. Given that goals are abstract ideas that are not immediately reached or attained, you need actual deeds (objectives) in order to accomplish the goals you have set. For example, the archives' goal may be to become better known in the city as a repository of X. To achieve this goal, you would then execute a series of actions (also known as objectives). For example:

- *Goal*: to be better known in the city as a repository of X.
- *Objectives*:
  - talk to other people in the field of X;
  - attend events in the city that have to do with X;
  - advertise in local/campus newspapers that you house collections about X.

As you can see, the statements listed under *Objectives* are actions, things to get done in order for the goal to be achieved. How many goals and objectives does your archival programme need? You can only decide that *after* you have established the mission and vision statements. You are (or are on your way to becoming) the expert of your archives. You will be the first to know what the archives' needs are and what you aspire for the archives to do and become.

Once you have completed or revised (if these already existed) the mission, vision and goals and objectives, you are ready to create the strategic plan. This is an important part of getting your archives organised.

Strategic planning

Before getting to the step-by-step process of creating your strategic plan, this section begins by answering a series of questions:

- *What is a strategic plan?* Strategic planning is management jargon for long-term future planning. Strategic planning refers to anything that will bring results from one to five years or more down the line. It is, however, only a map of the planning process, and can soon become outdated. Strategic plans must be revisited and updated every few years.

- *Do I really need one?* Yes, you really need one. Or at least it is highly recommend that you have such a plan. Once you have created a strategic plan, you will realise that it makes everything that happens in the archives uncomplicated.

- *What purpose do strategic plans serve?* Through the process of strategic planning you will determine where your archival programme is headed within the next year or three years or five years. The ultimate goal is to express how the programme will achieve all of its plans. It also establishes and highlights how the organisation's archival programme will know if it has achieved its projected goals or how much further it still needs to go.

Figure 2.1	Organisational chart sample

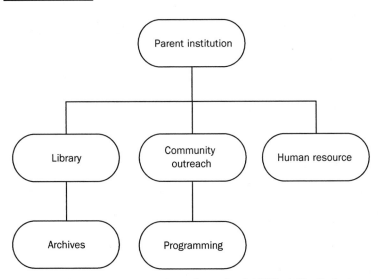

Note: Most microcomputer processing software (such MSWord, WordPerfect, etc.) now include a feature that will allow you to easily create an organisational chart such as this one.

Strategic planning made easier

Once you have your mission and vision statements settled, it will be helpful to incorporate them into the strategic plan. Creating the outline for the archives' success does not have to be difficult, dull or puzzling. The process here has been simplified and will take you through the steps to develop a clear path, set realistic goals and apply a programme to obtain them. In this chapter you are only given direct strategies to help you write a strategic plan. Though not obligatory, it is strongly recommended that you start with a basic organisational chart so you can see your archives' current position within the parent institution. Figure 2.1 shows a sample organisational chart that illustrates the chain or chains of command within an organisation.

A SWOT analysis is another part of the puzzle to creating a clear and intelligible strategic plan. SWOT stands for:

- S = strengths;
- W = weaknesses;
- O = opportunities;
- T = threats.

Some people really like to use the SWOT analysis as a guide to help them better lay out their strategic plan. SWOT analysis may make it easier to think of your organisation's present and future situation by forcing you to think in tangible directions.

Use the four SWOT categories to highlight the strengths and weaknesses of your archives. It is it extremely important that you honestly assess and recognise the weak points of the archives. In doing so, you have something to improve upon or to stop doing because the action is hurting the archives. On the S-list, list all that is going well and that you are going to strive to keep that way. On the W-list, list what can be improved on or what you do not possess. For example, if the archives lack a photocopier, state: 'The archives should have their own photocopier, so that materials are not removed from the premises'. The O-list is where you list the opportunities that you see for the archives to receive funding or better funding. Also list the real possibilities of doing special projects or possible grant application opportunities. This list can also serve as a place to transfer weaknesses. Weaknesses should be seen as opportunities. In fact, these are the archives' challenges. Finally, the T-list should include a list of all the threats you can imagine. Enumerate any and everything that may happen, which both could aid and negatively affect the archives before they actually happen. Examples of threats can be budget or staff shortcomings. These you want to be able to meet head on without surprises.[7] Appendix E provides a strategic plan SWOT layout sample.

After the SWOT analysis is complete, make sure that this tool helps you finalise those abstract sections of the strategic plan. Here are some tips for writing a strategic plan. The final version should address the following parts:

- Identify and/or clarify the vision and mission of the archives.

- Identify the essential or fundamental issues the archival programme must address to achieve its mission and goals, including internal and external influences that affect the archives.

- Develop a plan that reflects the archives' mission; then set the goals and objectives necessary to attain it.

- Schedule periodic evaluations to assess progress.

- Remind yourself and others that decisions and actions taken on behalf of the archives need to reflect the vision, mission and goals of the archives.[8]

When the strategic plan has been completed, make sure to stay on target as much as possible. This is why you schedule periodic reviews: to evaluate where you are. Otherwise, you will not be able to measure any outcomes of improvements or catch emerging challenges in a predictable manner. Appendix F provides a strategic plan outline.

Financial requirements for archiving on a budget

Setting your budget from the very beginning of your developing archives is very important. With a budget in hand you will be able to give your supervisor an estimate of how much it will cost to maintain the archives in their current state. Setting up a budget will help even if you are not given much money. If you are told to do an inventory of all the supplies you have available first, go ahead with that project. There may be more there than you think. When I did my informal survey of what I had for the library and archives, I discovered that I did not have to buy paper for the printer and copiers for at least six months. I also found hidden boxes with toner for both the printers and copier for the next five years – my predecessor obviously believed in purchasing in bulk. I share this anecdote to illustrate that although you may not end up receiving a very robust budget, you can still make ends meet with what you already have, or even find things that you did not know you had.

How to acquire more funding

At the beginning, make due with what you have. Make sure you have enough paper, folders, glue and other basic necessities for your archives to tide you over until you can have a serious talk with your supervisor. Being this frugal is acceptable. Your supervisor will know that you are indeed applying the *reduce, reuse and recycle* motto to the maximum as you are getting to know your archives' needs. Nevertheless, you will need to have funds allocated, no matter how small the amount. These funds need to be specifically set aside for the archives. At my library, I cut the budget for brochures by printing them in-house and adding that amount to my archives budget. I also hired students who had working grants, which meant that if I paid $7 an hour, the library actually only paid half and the grant paid the other half of the hourly pay. Stretching and acquiring funds can happen even if it means restructuring the current budget temporarily and in some instances permanently.

I increased the photocopying fee from 5 cents to 10 cents to match the rest of the university's copying fees. This proved to be a great money generator.

After you have made worthy efforts to prove why you need a budget and have demonstrated that you expend conservatively and on a needs basis only, then set up a meeting with your supervisor. A scheduled meeting will be taken more seriously than merely dropping by for a chat. This meeting, I guarantee you, will be much easier for you if you have already done the needs assessment study and written up the strategic plan. Why? Because not only have you, up to this point, managed the budget very carefully, but you have also projected what the archives can achieve and how this can benefit the parent institution.

Tips for saving on all aspects of the archives

Building and space maintenance

Try to maintain constant temperature and humidity. Not only is this extremely important for archival materials, but it is also a way for you to project monthly electricity costs that should remain constant. Although temperature and humidity control may not necessarily be under your control and this is often an expense that the archives do not incur, you should, nonetheless, at least investigate what the temperature and humidity is for your archives and whether they are being kept constant.

Processing and supplies

Supplies and staff time to process collections will be the most costly and ongoing expenditures you will have to deal with in order to get your collections processed in a timely manner. It is hoped that you will not have to stop processing a collection due to lack of supplies, but it can and does happen from time to time. If this should occur, try to see it in a positive way, as it will help you illustrate to your supervisor how the supply budget is connected to the processing of collections. Help them understand that there is more to archival processing than typing up an inventory list and making box labels. With the proper processing space, supplies and staff, your archives can only flourish. It is your responsibility to manoeuvre this frame of mind so that your peers and especially your supervisors, become your number one advocates.

Having learned from my predecessor, I too began purchasing in bulk, especially for archival materials, whenever possible. One costly, but well-worth expense was the purchase of a ~$250 acid-free tissue roll. The archivist and I made the decision that we were going to buy tissue paper once. By purchasing this roll we saved a lot of money in the long term because now we had at our disposal acid-free tissue paper that met the sizes of all of the materials we wished to interleaf (magazines, newspapers, maps, posters, pamphlets, etc.) by cutting the tissue to the needed size ourselves. Alternatively, if we had purchased tissue paper in specific sizes, which is sold in small amounts, we would never have been able to afford the rest of the archival supplies. As we were on a small budget, such an option was not cost-effective for us. Sized-tissue paper would have cost over $500. As it was, we spent less than half that.

Track your spending for all expenses. Keep folders with all receipts by types of material and make a note of price changes in supplies. If one vendor offers you a discount, mention it to your current suppliers. It may inspire them to try to keep you as a client by providing you with the discount you would have received from the other vendor. Many companies prefer that you do all of your purchasing online, so if you have an Internet connection, try shopping on the Web. Some vendors offer discounts on shipping or even free shipping when you order online. Check your paper catalogues too, for coupons or Internet discount codes and by all means use them. These coupons can translate into free shipping or up to 20 per cent discounts in some instances. Panel 2.2 provides tips for ordering supplies.

Panel 2.2: Tips for ordering supplies

Include the following supplies in your estimates:

- Acid-free document boxes (letter and legal size)
- Acid-free file folders (letter and legal size)
- Acid-free file labels
- Acid-free tissue paper roll
- Acid-free bond paper (for preservation photocopying)

If applicable, look for prices on microfilm boxes, long-playing (LP) record boxes, oversize boxes for maps, prints, etc.

When ordering archival boxes
The standard record storage box = 1 cubic foot approx.

1 cubic foot = 1 linear foot = Two 0.5 linear ft. document boxes

For example, if you have 30 banker's boxes = 30 cubic feet

30 cubic feet = 60 document boxes

One document box can hold between 10–30 folders depending on the materials housed in the box.

Staffing

If possible, try to hire support staff subsidised through government grants. Hiring staff at low wages goes against the living wage philosophy, so another option is to create a part-time position at a higher hourly wage and making sure that you only hire the most competent person for the job, so you receive your money's worth. To keep your staff happy, be sure to train them well and inform them clearly of expectations. Time well spent at the beginning will cut down on time and money later as you will not have to spend additional time constantly retraining staff. Do, however, provide refresher workshops as a continuing education opportunity for your staff. Revisiting difficult or detailed procedures will greatly aid in keeping in mind proper archival protocols of processing and detract from shortcuts of any type. For example, once a year you could have a refresher workshop on customer service or how to store fragile materials. In time, you will see where your staff needs refreshing and can tailor workshops to the more difficult tasks. Keeping your staff well trained will maintain good morale in the workplace and improve overall performance.

External money sources

Contrary to popular belief, neither grant writing nor fundraising is less time-consuming than the other. They are both equally time-consuming and they are also two of the most common ways to get external funds for an archival programme.

Grants

Applying for grants can become your full-time job if you are not careful to limit your activities in this area, especially if you have to run the archives and write grants. If grant writing is one of your primary duties, make sure that this is clear to your supervisors. Otherwise, it can become a major issue if they think you are not spending enough time on your other duties. Educate your supervisors about how much time is required for you to do all your duties and point out the fact that if you need to write grants, your other duties may suffer. But do not let this become a dire predicament. Make it clear that you want to fulfil all of your duties, but realistically there is no way that everything can be done within your working week if you are the only one running the archives. From experience, it takes a minimum of 20 solid hours to write a good grant proposal. This is not counting research before you start writing or the time spent filling out applications.

The process begins with seeking grant sources. This is time-consuming because you need to be well-informed before you start dedicating the time necessary to writing a good grant proposal. Where you look for sources depends on what type of archives you have and what type of funds you are seeking. Many places, such as governmental agencies and private foundations, can be found on the Internet – there used to be directories of fund-granting institutions but they are fast becoming obsolete due to Internet sites. Some examples of funds granting organisations for archives are the *National Historical Publications and Records Commission*, in the USA and the *South East Museum, Library and Archives Council* in the UK.

Once you win a grant, do not necessarily expect that you will receive the full award, as the parent institution may well deduct some, due to costs such as overheads and maintenance. This varies from organisation to organisation. Do ask the person in charge of distributing the funds at your institution to give you an idea of how much money the archives would really receive if a certain amount were won. This way, you can plan accordingly.

As it is well-known, desperate times call for desperate measures. Depending on the type of institution you are working in, you should try to encourage co-workers in other departments, for example, to include the archives in their grant proposals. Have a small percentage be directed to the fund for archives maintenance, as the archives could have been or may be in the future a source of information for them. At some point, the archives will enhance their research process or archives staff will help them find information for their projects. Likewise, do have people in your organisation who have a need for the collections in their research add a line for archival expenses or maintenance to their grant proposals.

Fundraising

You will have to be creative when it comes to fundraising. One idea that worked great for me, when in a bind to come up with new sources of funding, was to have a used book sale. I invited my co-workers at the centre to donate books to sell so that we could raise funds for the archives. The funds were specifically geared to the purchase of acid-free archival materials. The archivist at the time, Marisol Ramos, donated her rather large paperback science fiction collection so that funds could be raised. Her donation to the used book sale soon inspired many others at the centre to also donate books, so that more funds could be raised. Even our supervisor, after hearing how well the sale was going, donated books from his office bookcase. This is not meant to imply that you should sell the books from your collection, but if multiple copies abound you could consider putting a few titles up for sale.

Other ideas

Have other people fundraise for you. Consider starting a 'Friends of the Archives' group as a way to inspire donors to make a monetary contribution to help buy supplies to process the archives' collections. For example, donations from users/visitors may be elicited by suggesting to them to have their friends or families send a monetary gift instead of buying a store gift for them. Advertise that you take donations in honour of family and friends for special occasions such as birthdays, weddings, graduations and memorials for loved ones.

All of these little bits add up. By the way, the used book sale generated enough funds for us to buy more acid-free boxes and finally finish transferring all of the archives' materials into sturdy new acid-free boxes. Everything in this section is based on personal experience and all of the suggestions have been employed successfully. Imagination and backbone will help you create a thriving archival programme.

Notes

1. See: *http://oregonstate.edu/instruct/anth370/gloss.html* (accessed: 20 November 2005).
2. See: *www.cdc.gov/tobacco/evaluation_manual/glossary.html* (accessed: 20 November 2005).
3. Tashakkori and Teddlie (2003: 711).
4. Fink and Kosecoff (1998: 1).
5. Vogt (1993: 184).
6. See McNamara (1999) at: *http://www.managementhelp.org/plan_dec/str_plan/stmnts.htm* (accessed: 22 December 2005) and Alliance for Nonprofit Management (year unknown) at: *http://www.allianceonline.org/FAQ/strategic_planning/what_s_in_vision_statement.faq* (accessed: 22 December 2005).

7. See The Coaching Lounge (year unknown) at: *http://thecoachinglounge.com/strategicplanning.html* (accessed: 12 December 2005).

8. See Swinton (year unknown) at: *http://www.trans4mind.com/ counterpoint/swinton3.shtml* (accessed: 12 December 2005).

Archival roadmap: practical considerations when writing archival policies

Setting archival policy is another major key to establishing a successful archival programme. Writing these policies will ensure standardisation of practices and procedures, clarify the chain of command and place you in the position to control the direction of the archival programme for years to come. This section provides practical advice to apply when writing your policies.

Collection development policy

The purpose of a collection development policy is to lay out the rationale, guidelines and particulars of why the archives focus on a particular area of expertise. You want to be able to answer the following questions:

- Why do we collect?
- What do we collect?
- Why do we select some materials while we reject others? And,
- Who do we collect for?

This is a necessary and vital document to deal with administrators, funding agencies, donors and users alike. If your archival procedures are questioned, this policy will point out the basis of your method of procedure. If donors bring materials that may be improper for your archives, this policy will provide a graceful way to say *no* and will also educate your donors on what is accepted at your archives. This experience may even direct them to the right depository for their materials. Funding agencies will take you more seriously if you can show them that you are in control of your archives and that you have a mission that they may want to support.

Components for a collection development policy

Rationale

At the beginning of your policy, you will place the vision, mission and goals and objectives that you developed while creating the archives' strategic plan. This is the *raison d'être* of your archival endeavour. This section answers the question 'Why do we collect materials on X?'

The core

- *Purpose*: What is the purpose of the archives? In a brief and concise matter explain what the archives document. For example, life experiences, historical periods, events, ethnic community and/or individuals (e.g. poets, writers).

- *User community*: Who is your audience? List current and future users. Define your audience (e.g. scholars, primary and secondary students, faculty, general public).

- *Scope of coverage*: List subject areas, geographical area, languages, chronological limits, date of publications, type of materials and exclusions (what is not collected).

- *Collections housed in archival repositories*: List the location of collections if placed in more than one room or building.

- *Cooperative collection development*: Any agreements/ policies with other departments that share the collections.

- *Statements on resource sharing*: Agreements/policies with other similar institutions.

- *Procedures for reviewing collection development policy*: Summarise procedures for revision decided in the strategic plan document.

Summaries of all archival policies at your institution

- *Summary of acquisition/donation policy*: Identify who is responsible for creating and implementing this policy. List the required criteria to acquire and/or accept donations. Indicate if there are procedures to accept feedback from other stakeholders of the archives regarding what other materials should be considered for you to collect.

- *Summary of access policy*: In one statement, summarise access policy. For example, hours of service, who can gain access to use the materials (clientele), etc.

- *Summary of deaccessioning policy*: List criteria used to deaccession a collection. For example, improper focus, mouldy materials, multiple copies, etc.

Appendix G presents the archives policy template.

Acquisition/donation policy

The precarious financial situation of most archives does not allow for institutions to set acquisition budgets. Therefore, receiving and soliciting collections as donations to the archives are the most common practices. Due to these practices the archives need to have a written policy governing future acquisitions. This document can be used as a marketing tool when discussing with donors why your institution's archives is the ideal place for their personal papers to be donated. Most importantly, the donation policy should reflect the decisions made when devising the collection development policy.

Components for the creation of an acquisition/donation policy

Mission of the archives

Insert the mission statement of the archives. This serves as a reminder of the purpose of the archives for administrators and outsiders.

Definition of archival appraisal

Include a brief definition of archival appraisal to set the tone for the rest of the donation policy. See it as an opportunity to educate your stakeholders about the principles that govern your archival practices. For example, you can use William J. Maher's (1992: 36) definition:

> [A]ppraisal – the process by which the archivist assesses the value of documents and decides which should be kept and which should be destroyed.

Statement of responsibility

- Clearly state who has the legal authority to set policy.

- Who is in charge of making acquisition decisions?

- If more than one person is in charge of making decisions, include a brief explanation of the chain of command and how this applies to different types of donations.

Evaluation criteria

List what factors are used to accept or reject donations. The following criteria can be adapted to your needs:

- Expand the current collection.

- Meet the research needs of the archives' clientele.

- The collection falls within the collecting areas specified in the collection development policy.

- The archives has the funding and storage space to properly care for the collection.

- The donor is legally entitled to transfer ownership of the materials.

- There are no other archival institutions bidding for the same collection.

In addition, use examples to describe the type of materials that you accept and reject to make it easier for donors to know what to bring when delivering donated materials. For example:

- The archives accept:
  - personal and family papers;
  - letters/correspondence;
  - diaries/memoirs/reminiscences;
  - speeches/lectures.

- The archives do not accept:
  - albums/scrapbooks;
  - newspapers.

Acquisitions guidelines

- Explain the protocol for accepting a donation (the chain of command).
- Explain the archives' position regarding restricted donations (e.g. the archives do not accept donations with undue restrictions to access).
- Explain procedures when soliciting donations (e.g. phone solicitations, letter requests, press releases).
- Weeding rules (e.g. discard multiples copies, dispose of pest-infested materials).

Transfer of materials (deed of gift)

- Provide a definition for deed of gift.
- Explain the process of transferring ownership of the collection.
- Inform where forms may be obtained (e.g. archivist's office, development office).
- Add statement related to accepting donations for deposit (e.g. the archives generally do not accept materials on deposit or on loan).

Restrictions

Explain the archives' position in regards to donor-imposed restrictions on access (e.g. prohibiting access to certain parts of the collection for 20 years or until the death of the donor).

Copyright statement

Statement related to copyright ownership of a collection. Mention what the legal means are for transferring copyright to the archives.

Purchases (archives' position)

State what the archives' position is on purchasing collections (e.g. the archives discourage the practice of purchasing donations to avoid the practice of 'archives-shopping', or offering a collection for sale or donation to multiple archives at the same time).

See Appendix H for the acquisitions policy template.

Archival access policy

Providing access to your collections is one of the fundamental goals of the archives. The nature of archival materials, though, makes access a more complex task than it is in libraries. Your access policy will vary according to your situation (such as small staff, restrictions from donors, lack of duplication devices, etc.) Again, your policy is the tool to instruct users of the services, limitations and proper protocol for accessing a collection. In contrast with libraries, archival access is not a right; it is a privilege. It is a privilege because damage to the materials is irreversible and, in most cases, impossible to recover. These considerations need to be balanced with the principle of *equality of access*. Your policy should ensure that all users are treated equally and there cannot be special rules that favour one user over another in terms of access to any collections in your custody. Setting this policy early on will greatly help you offer access to your users without damaging your archives' unique documents.

Components for the creation of an access policy

- Comments on collection care and how it relates to access. Introduce the policy with a statement of how the materials are housed, how they have been processed, access to finding aids, etc.
- Type of services (e.g. by appointment, e-mail, telephone).
- Authorised users (e.g. bona fide researchers, graduate students).
- Level of access. What are the conditions to allow access to archives users?
  - access to reading room;
  - permission to photocopy materials;
  - permission to quote from a document;
  - publication rights for documents, photographs and any other archival material.
- Reading room rules (e.g. photocopy services, such as provide copyright permission forms, releases, cost per photocopy).
- Restrictions on access (e.g. no access to unprocessed materials; limited access or no access to donations with specific restrictions, such as date of opening, confidentiality and privacy issues).
- Hours of operation.
- Preferred citation.

See Appendix I for the access policy template.

Deaccessioning policy

Even after adhering faithfully to your collection development policy, you may still need to deaccession collections. There are many reasons for the practice: to remove items of little relevance, untrustworthy or in poor condition; to rid a collection of inferior material; clerical errors, lack of space and/or the cost of maintenance or storage. It is a controversial policy because many users believe that archives do not throw anything away. This is a misconception that endures even though it contradicts the idea of archives as repositories of unique items. Therefore, it is necessary to explain clearly why, when and how such a drastic step is to be taken. This practice should not be confused with weeding a collection while processing it. Deaccessioning and weeding are two different processes. When we *deaccession*, we permanently remove an entire collection from the archives, while *weeding* is part of the process of cleaning, processing and describing a collection. Here then are the sections necessary for your policy.

Components for the creation of a deaccessioning policy

- *Statement of responsibility*: State clearly the chain of command when making a decision to deaccession (e.g. archivist → immediate supervisor → director).

- *Definitions and examples*: Because deaccessioning is such a controversial practice, always include a simple and clear definition and some examples to illustrate how the policy is applied.

- *Rationale*: Explain in layman's terms why materials may be deaccessioned – this is one of the most sensitive topics when dealing with donors. Clearly state that this is a policy of last resort.

- *Guidelines*: List deaccessioning criteria, such as:
  - physical condition: brittleness, mould, water damage;
  - collection development and/or institutional decision: unclear legal title or ownership, issues of accuracy, authority or authenticity, unfitness to current or revised collection policy.

- *Right of first refusal*: If the donors specified in the deed of gift have the *right of first refusal*, always try to contact the donor to inform them if their donation will be deaccessioned or if you plan to remove a great amount of materials while processing a collection.

- *Procedures*: Establish a deaccessioning action plan that clearly defines when and how materials will be discarded. (See Appendix J for the deaccessioning sample scenarios).

- List forms that need to be filled out to keep a record of materials removed from the archives.

See Appendices K and L for the deaccessioning policy sample and template.

Writing policies does not need to be a time-consuming and difficult process. It is really the gathering of common sense and best practices. It is also the underpinning of your entire archival practices and a roadmap for anyone to follow after you are no longer running the archives.

Getting to the core:
You created your archives –
now what?

The day-to-day business of archives does not seem like a very exciting job but the decisions we make now will have far-reaching consequences well into the future. If you do not want people 20 years from now to think unkindly of your actions, take your time to cogitate how you plan to run the archival practice and activities. As Sue McKemmish (1999: 10) explained in the essay collection *Keeping Archives*:

> ...the meaning and value of archives derive from the social and organisational context in which they were created and used and from their links with other records. Used or interpreted out of context, their significance is lost or compromised. Therefore, to provide for their continuing useability [sic], archivists manage archives from their creation in ways which preserve their meaning and value as well as ensuring their long-term survival.

Our job is not only to organise the archives, but to also protect and preserve the context within which the records were created. Collections are like archaeological excavations. You may wonder: How so? Archaeological excavations encompass a specific space and time. The objects found inside an excavation – as in an archival collection – were created by an individual or group of individuals. Each particular object/record has significance only based on where it was located among the layers of soil/paper/folders (which tell us the time and place of its creation) and how it is connected with other objects found in the excavation/collection. An object or document, taken out of context, loses its value (be it evidential, informative or historical). It is our job to safeguard both the *context* and *content* of the collections entrusted to the archives.

The following sections discuss the different aspects of archival work and tips on how to incorporate them into your daily routine. Most of the advice provided in these sections applies to small, subject-oriented archives, instead of institutional ones, but the concepts can be adapted to organisational archives as well.

Appraisal

Appraisal is an evaluation tool to determine whether a collection should be acquired and preserved for the long term by an archival institution. If a donor approaches the archives to offer a collection, suggest a visit to where the collection is currently located to examine it and begin the appraisal process. Alternatively, be proactive and target archival donors in advance and offer them a free appraisal to assist them in identifying the place that can best safeguard their collections. Whatever the situation, keep documentation (see Appendix M for the prospective donor form template) on when, who and what collections you are tracking for the archives.

The main idea behind this action is to identify in advance what materials would be appropriate for your archives and to inform the potential donor of what materials you cannot keep and offer suggestions of where to take them and what to do with them. At this point you want to be seen as a resource for donors and eventually as a first choice when they are thinking of placing their materials in your custody. In an ideal world, appraisal would happen before the collection was accepted. Sometimes, however, you will not have a choice in the matter, as the donor may come to the archives with all of their boxes. Regardless of the circumstances, the tools offered here will be useful, as you can start the process of appraisal straight away. But *do not* accept a donation without having the donor sign a deed of gift (see Chapter 5 to learn how to create this important form).

To facilitate your job while appraising, here are some of the tools that I used, tweaked and created while working as an archivist. Some of them, such as the acquisition guidelines, have already been discussed, but the rest are practical applications of archival principles.

Acquisition guidelines

Bring these with you when interviewing and inspecting a collection. Have them available at your office or front desk. Take the time to explain to potential donors what the archival programme collects (subjects, types of materials, time period, significant individuals, etc.) and why other materials are not collected. Offer references to other archival institutions that may be more appropriate for a particular collection.

Appraisal survey

Surveys are excellent tools when assessing the archival value of a collection. They are also useful for both the archivist and the donor to understand the archival appraisal decision process. By employing a simple survey while interviewing your donor, you can identify issues that concern you, which can be resolved even before the collection arrives at the archives. To create this survey, concepts such as authenticity, provenance, reliability and relevance are combined with some of Theodore R. Schellenberg's (1956) primary and secondary values (administrative value, evidential value and informational value) of documents. In addition, two more factors are included: intrinsic/historic value and monetary value (for insurance purposes only). Both of these have an impact on appraisal. (See Appendix N for the appraisal survey template).

Using your guidelines and the survey form, you can provide an opportunity to involve donors in the appraisal process and educate them about the role you play for the archives.

Acquisition/selection

Most small archives and non-profit organisations tend to acquire their collections more by accident than by design. Somebody may drop off a box of books; another person may deliver several boxes about some event they or their grandparents participated in that may or not be related to your institution. A board member, director, executive or officer planning retirement may say to you: 'You know, I am retiring, would you like my papers?' Sometimes, people even leave boxes outside your archives with stuff they think someone would like to keep. And all of a sudden, when you least expect it, you have an archival programme underway.

Whenever possible, be proactive. Regardless of how your archives started, you can take control of their destiny by:

- creating a policy (as discussed in Chapter 3);
- identifying and contacting your potential donors;
- sending potential donors a copy of your acquisition guidelines;
- inviting potential donors to visit your facility and giving them a tour;
- Follow-up! Follow-up! Follow-up! (Use the prospective donor form found in Appendix M).

Unless you have unlimited amounts of money, it is better to discourage buying collections. Small archives cannot compete with big, well-funded institutions that can afford to purchase 'diamond-studded' collections. More worrisome, though, is the recent trend of selling historical and/or collectible items on eBay and other online auction sites. It is distressing to see materials that in the past would have been donated to an archival programme, being sold off to the highest bidder online. Collections are broken up and its pieces sold, not for their historical value but for their collectible value, without consideration of context. It is a practice that probably will continue and there is little that archivists can do about it. The best advice we can give you is to continue cultivating relationships with donors and prospective donors. Encourage them to donate. If your country/state provides tax deductions and/or incentives for donations to non-profit institutions, advertise this fact to your donors and educate them on how to take advantage of these incentives. In the end, it is in your hands to shape the way your archives grow. It is important to recognise that this will occur through well-planned acquisition practices.

As a proactive archival staff, take control of acquisition decisions. Ask yourself the following questions when deciding to acquire a collection:

- Does the collection enhance your current holdings?

- Does the subject matter of the collection fall under the acquisition guidelines?

- Is the donor legally entitled to donate the collection?

- Can your archives properly store and preserve the collection?

- Does the donation include a monetary grant to cover processing?

As you gain experience doing the job, you can add more questions to this basic list and further develop your criteria by adapting the questions to the changing needs of your institution.

The fine art of donor relations

The lifelong relationship between archives and donors

The relationship between archives and donors can be likened to a marriage. It is a lifetime commitment and you are not only 'marrying' your donor but you are also inheriting his or her family. Donors may be sometimes forgotten because the emphasis tends to fall on the collection, on its subjects and themes and on the individual or groups represented in it. This is especially true if the collection was not processed as soon as it was received.

My first challenge as a professional archivist was to track donors. When I started my collection inventory, I found that there was no documentation on when, who and how the materials had been acquired. Some of the donations had been received 30 years ago and no one knew why or how things came in. With the use of some sleuthing skills acquired in library school – and a lot of luck – I was able to track six of the ten donors who had donated materials between 1970 and 1990.

Although it was a time-consuming process, in the long run it was a blessing in disguise, because it provided me with the opportunity to re-connect with these forgotten donors. Exchanging recollections about when and why they had donated their materials to the archives gave them opportunity to strengthen their relationship as donors with me, the archivist.

This experience gave me much to ponder regarding the relationship between donors and archives. When archival theory and management was discussed in library school, the idea of donor relations was barely glossed over. Creators are more present in archival sciences because the archival principles of provenance and original order are based on the actions of creators. However, we did not dedicate much time to talking about donors in class. Working in the real world, I find that, donors are fundamental to the wellbeing of an archival programme, especially if you consider that not all creators are donors and not all donors are creators. Archives can receive donations from creators, but these gifts may also come from family members, friends or total strangers who just happened to enjoy collecting materials about someone or something.

Of all of your stakeholders, donors are the lifeblood of the archives and they are worth cultivating before, during and after they have donated materials. We need them as much as they need us because they are our partners when working on implementing the archives acquisition policy. We want to find collections that fit the archives, while donors want to find a caring place for their collections. So, it is a mutually beneficial association.

Our relationship with donors also has long-lasting effects. They can spread a good (or bad) word about you and your archives and attract other donors with related materials that can potentially enrich your holdings. In the non-profit world, donors may be part of a board of directors as well: another group of your stakeholders. Most importantly, building high-quality relationships with your donors establishes a sense of respect and cooperation that can last for decades. You need to build trust with your donors to avoid misunderstandings and to explain such things as deaccessioning or the reasons for not accepting a collection. Furthermore, reassuring donors about the manner in which your archives will manage their donations may avoid unreasonable restrictions that can hamper the accessibility of the collections for future users. Therefore, regardless of who your donors are, your archival programme should always keep track of them and their heirs. Here are some suggestions on how to work with donors and their gifts:

- Start a collection file for the donor when first contacted. Your first record should be the prospective donor form.
- Keep the original deed of gift and any other legal documentation regarding the donation.
- Keep updated contact information, not only of the donor but also of his/her family, known heirs or the executor of the estate (See Appendix O for the donor registry template).
- Send letters informing the donor and their family of exhibits and related events that will involve using the collection's materials.
- Keep the relationship alive!

Establishing good relationships with donors and their families and associates is an investment that will pay off for many years. Do not forget them after they drop off their collections!

Drafting deeds of gift

A deed of gift is a legal contract between the archival programme and a donor(s) regarding the physical and intellectual transfer of a collection to your institution. This vital document must be part of your records documenting the donation. One of the challenges at my previous archival job was to obtain deeds of gifts for collections donated 30 years ago that had never been legally transferred to the archives. As our programme had few resources, we could not take the chance of processing collections that we did not own and could therefore be taken away from us at a later time. The cost of processing a collection is quite high if you consider how expensive archival supplies are, as well as the salaries and time of your archival staff. Some people thought that I was exaggerating the situation and wasting my time trying to obtain these agreements. They assumed that if the collections were already at the archives, we must own them, right? One of my archival mentors always told the following anecdote when discussing the need for deeds of gift: Archives 'A' processed a collection from a well-reputed author. They advertised that the collection was available and that they were exhibiting some of the most interesting materials in their special collection. The grandson of the writer, who was the heir and executor of his grandfather's estate, learned of the plans of Archives 'A' and was outraged. The grandson felt that his grandfather's papers should be in Archives 'B', with which he had a good relationship and where he had already placed his own personal papers. He sent his lawyers to demand the withdrawal of the collection from Archives 'A' and its transfer to Archives 'B'. Seeking to defend its right to own this collection, the archivist in charge of Archives 'A' went searching for the deed of gift in the collection files, but alas! There were no documents to be found. Not a letter or deed or even a postcard stating that the original donor wanted his donation in Archives 'A'. With no evidence and unable to survive a lawsuit, Archives 'A' had to relinquish *its* donation to the writer's heir. The moral of this story is obvious: *always* have your donors sign a deed of gift. This is a true story and I have taken it to heart whenever I have worked as an archivist.

If possible, ask the legal department of your institution to create a deed of gift document for you. Consult with them regarding the legal requirements needed to make official the physical and intellectual transfer of the collection. You want to create a document that has the following characteristics:

- The terms of the agreement need to be clear. Avoid using very legalistic language.
- If you already have a deed of gift, contact the institution's legal department to determine whether the document has been written properly.
- Print the name(s) of the parties involved in the transaction.
- Include the date of the transaction.
- Explain what type of transfer you are receiving, e.g. physical, copyright or both.
- Include any applicable restrictions.
- State what the archives will do with the donation after acquiring it.
- State the process of 'first refusal' in case the collection needs to be deaccessioned.
- Include the signatures of the donor(s) and the authorised official accepting the donation.

See Appendices P and Q for sample deeds of gift.

The price you pay for not having clear ownership of your collection is its possible loss by irate, unhappy or disgruntled heirs that may have different ideas of where and how 'their' collection should be managed.

Ethical considerations

Ethics are an essential element when dealing with donors. In our eagerness to make a collection available at our archives, we may sometimes find ourselves walking the fine line between ethical and unethical behaviour. I remember attending an archival panel on 'cooperation among archives and the community' a few years ago. Even though there were great discussions about cooperative projects between archivists and local community organisations, the discussion that elicited the most passionate reaction was the one on the practice of 'bidding against other archives'. This is an unethical practice frowned upon by many archivists but still practised by some archives in many parts of the world. Based on the reactions from many of the attendants at the conference, I could tell that even though this practice is considered unethical, it is still a problem that needs to be dealt with in our everyday work. There are many practices that fall under unethical behaviour, such as overstating the monetary value of collections, accepting unreasonable restrictions (for example restricting access to an individual for personal reasons of the donor or the archivist) or disregarding the donor's wishes stated in a deed of gift. You may be committed to conducting your archival practices in an ethical matter but still encounter some situations that can place you in a very uncomfortable position. When this occurs, what can you do about it?

To avoid some of these unethical situations at your archives you may want to engage your stakeholders (potential donors, current donors, supervisors) in a dialogue about your professional organisation's code of ethics. Most professional archival organisations have a code of ethics that serves as a moral compass when dealing with donors, collections and archives. As with your policies and guidelines, you can use a code of ethics to educate your stakeholders on the appropriate, ethical and even legal procedures related to acquiring and managing archival collections. Even though codes of ethics are not legally enforceable, in a moral sense, they can support you when dealing with a difficult situation.

A word of caution: You may be placed in circumstances where taking an ethical stand may jeopardise your position. The only advice I can give you is to follow your conscience and do what you think is right. When that is not possible, keep documentation that establishes your point of view and the fact that you acted on others' instructions. Pick your battles and do what you feel is right, proper and ethical. There will always be politics, even in archives, and sometimes you can only do your best.

Workspace and preservation with limited or no budget

Setting up the proper workspace for processing and a facility for preserving collections can be a very expensive proposition for new archives and archives with limited budgets. In this chapter, you are first presented with two scenarios illustrating an archival programme's 'absolute minimum requirements' and 'minimal facilities and equipment of the properly functioning archives'. Then you are presented with a third option. This third scenario is the one that makes it viable to set up your workplace and preservation plan when you find yourself in a limited or no budget predicament.

As the majority of us fall into this latter scenario at the beginning of our endeavour, most of this chapter is dedicated to it. The other two, nonetheless, serve as guidelines to aspire to once your archives have flourished.

Scenario 1: the ideal setting

This scenario describes the absolute minimum requirements for the archives, when you have a full and ideal budget. These so-called 'absolute minimum requirements' are for an archival programme that, realistically, few of us may have. Nevertheless, this is what most of us will be spending our time and energy striving for. As can be seen from Panel 6.1, these

Panel 6.1: Absolute minimum requirements

Allocation space recommended for archival facilities

Records storage/stacks	60–70%
Archival services and administration	30–40%
Processing areas (closed to the public)	15–22%
Reference areas/exhibits and public conveniences	7–10%
Administrative offices (semi-closed to the public)	8%

Absolute minimum requirements for facilities and equipment

Areas closed to the public

Storage area

Environment:

- Clean
- Cold +18–20°C
- Dry (no less than 45–55% relative humidity)
- Dark

Equipment:

- Shelves
- Fire detectors and extinguishers
- Ladders/step stools
- Trolleys (hand trucks, dolly, carts)
- Thermohygrograph

Processing area

Environment:

- No direct sun
- Free of dust

Public areas

Reading room

Environment:

- Around +22°C

Equipment:

- A table and chair per researcher
- Bookcases
- Copy machine (share with office)
- Microfilm readers

Exhibition area

Environment:

- Low light level if original material exhibited

Equipment:

- Fire detectors and extinguishers
- Display cabinets

Equipment:

- Brush or vacuum cleaner
- Workbench
- Shelves, racks, cupboards

Supplies:

- Boxes
- Cotton tape
- Wrapping paper
- Folders
- Envelopes
- Plastic clips

Administrative areas

Environment:

- Around +22°C

Space:

- 3.3 square metres per member of staff

Equipment:

- A desk and chair per member of staff
- Bookcase
- Telephone
- Word processing equipment

- Screens
- Chairs or lounge

Seminar training

Environment:

- Around +22°C

Equipment:

- Blinds or heavy curtains to exclude light
- A table and chair per researcher
- Black/whiteboard
- Slide projector
- Screen
- Overhead projector
- Film projector
- Video equipment

Source: Ellis (1999: 52–3)

are clearly ideal conditions – if these requirements had to be met before starting, most of us would not have an archival programme at all. Most of us have to create archives within the space given and rarely are we granted new or additional space (or it can take quite a while). Therefore, if a functional archive is to be created efficiently, reconfiguring and maximising the use of available space is essential. To achieve what some archivists consider the minimum, you need to spend a lot of money. If this is the absolute minimum, we can only wonder what the maximum might be.

Scenario 2: properly functioning archives

Panel 6.2 illustrates the 'minimal facilities and equipment' to set up 'properly functioning archives', assuming you have a very good budget. Although just as long as the first list and with many things in common, this second list is not the absolute minimum and is thus open to other possibilities. The list is also self-explanatory, mentioning not only why you need something like shelving, but giving the type of shelving it should be or how these shelves should be adjustable to accommodate boxes of different sizes and weights. Our third scenario's physical space set-up adapts many of the recommendations from this second scenario because it acknowledges that the size and development of archives programmes vary. No square metres are given per staff person, making it easier to adapt the space you have.

Scenario 3: the little or no budget plan

This scenario best describes when you are just starting out and creating an archival programme where none previously

Panel 6.2: Facilities and equipment

A. Facilities

1. General considerations for archives facilities:

   (a) The archives should be located in a fire-resistant or fireproof building and equipped with fire extinguishers.

   (b) Temperature and humidity conditions should be maintained as constant as possible. As most archives store many different types of material together, each with different optimum storage conditions, it will be impossible to provide ideal conditions for all material.

   Suggested ranges:

   - Temperature: 60–70°F (16–21°C)

   - Relative Humidity: 40–50%

   - Fluctuations within the suggested ranges these should be minimised.

   (c) All archives areas should be provided with locks. Access to keys to these should be strictly limited.

   (d) The archives should be equipped with a heat and smoke detector system and preferably a water detector system.

   (e) The archive should be protected by a security alarm system.

   (f) If there are windows in the archives, they should be covered with ultraviolet screening and heavily curtained.

(g) If fluorescent lighting is used in the archives it should be covered with ultraviolet filter screens, particularly in display areas and areas in which archival material is stored on open shelves.

(h) The archives should be located in an area with convenient access to a loading dock.

(i) The archives should be located in an area with convenient access to running water.

2. Consideration for a reading room for researchers where access and use may be supervised and restricted:

(a) The reading room should be easily accessible to the stacks.

(b) The reading room should accommodate several users.

(c) The reading room should be well lighted and furnished with appropriate furniture. This furniture should not provide the opportunity for the concealment of archival material.

(d) The reading room should also contain guides to the collection; a desk and a chair for supervisory personnel; an area for checking book bags, briefcases and coats; and an area to register users.

3. Considerations for other area requirements:

(a) Archives require a stack area which can be limited to archives personnel. The size of the stack area will be determined by the present size of the holdings and the volume of annual accessions.

(b) An area must be provided for the processing of unorganised collections. This area should be physically separated from the reading area and preferably from the stack area. A regular office may often serve this function. It should be provided with shelving, a large flat table, chair and enough space to accommodate the staff and supplies used in processing.

B. Equipment

1. Shelving should be provided for present holdings plus five years projected accessions.

2. Preferably, the shelving should be metal with adjustable metal shelves of adequate width and load-bearing capacity.

3. Special storage equipment for oversize items such as large photographs, maps and blueprints should be provided, as well as appropriate filing cabinets as needed.

4. Acid-free covered document cases; both legal and letter size

5. Acid-free file folders, both legal and letter size

6. Records storage or transfer cartons

7. Catalogue cards

8. Typewriters or computer with printer

9. Equipment for transporting containers

10. Clerical supplies and equipment

Source: Maher (1992: 386–7)

existed. Unfortunately, once we have fallen into this scenario at the beginning, it is also where we may remain for a long time thereafter. Here then is advice for setting up the physical spaces. There is nothing more important than realising that you need to work with the resources that you are given. There is no other way around it. You cannot afford to wait until the day when you have achieved all of the required conditions to create the ideal archives. So let us begin.

Scan your archives area. Ask yourselves these questions:

- Can you make more space?
- How are you using your allotted space?
- How can you maximise furniture and equipment already available in your given space/s?

In the storage area, you should place materials and all of your collections not in use. They should only be out when requested by researchers or if the materials are being processed by you or your staff. As with the requirements for ideal archives, if these requirements had to be met beforehand it would be a long time before most of us had any archives in place.

Setting up the physical space

Under this plan you work with what you have and, most importantly, prioritise your plan of action. The first step is to measure and maximise the space given. From this, you can then make a budget for purchasing cabinets of different sizes, boxes, paper, pens and general archival and office supplies. Do not be embarrassed to ask for furniture in the beginning or if you see that a piece of furniture is being underutilised in some other area of the organisation or even in another department. Make sure people know you need a long but narrow working table, a small chair or that you are willing to trade three large chairs for two small ones. Just get creative – all of your furniture needs may be around the building. Ours were – all we needed to buy was wire shelving.

To set up your space, first you have to know whether it is your permanent space or whether you will be able to move materials to a newly-designated archival storage space. However, even if it is a temporary facility you will still have to work with what you have been given. For example, we had to work with one long and narrow room. In order to maximise space, shelving was set up high along one wall only. The desk and working table were across from each other further down the wall from the shelving. Measure your space so that you can reconfigure and maximise the space you have. Remember, space does not expand or grow. You must work with what you were allocated as working and storage space. You do not need to worry about the access issues for the reading room until you actually need it, and you may come up with other options in the meantime.

A good space is dry, with stable temperature and humidity, has shelving and some filing cabinets. If these basics are not met, you can still work and get started. But these are issues that will have to be dealt with sooner or later. One of our issues was the temperature control which kept changing of its own accord. Due to the lack of a constant temperature, the room had a small but steady leak. Later we discovered the culprit: a faulty air-conditioning installation that had occurred when the whole building had been seismically retrofitted a few years before any of us had been hired.

If possible, obtain access to running water or have a sink in the archives processing area. Why, you may ask? Clean hands are of the essence when working with delicate materials. You may also, at times, have to work with special adhesives, and having a sink nearby enables you to wash your hands while being able to watch the materials glue together. You will not be out of sight or gone at all before the adhesive sets. It is important to have a sink if you will be doing a lot of preservation work. Lacking one initially, as we did, may be counterbalanced by using moistened wipes.

In an ideal world, you would have unlimited space. But, realistically, I have yet to see an archival programme get unlimited space and proper storage for the collections and materials within it from the very beginning. The only exceptions are national archives or very large museums, which are government-funded agencies that receive what they need to properly function. Remember, there are always options to consider, especially when you are on a budget.

Preservation on a budget

It is hard not to feel guilty when most archival manuals tell us to transfer everything over into acid-free folders and boxes. But if you are on a budget, you may not have enough money to buy preservation supplies. Do not feel ashamed to work with what you have. There are many low-budget options when you are starting an archival programme and resources are limited. Keep in mind, however, that these are only temporary solutions. Build on your experiences and identify the areas that need support from your supervisors and donors. Archives do not live on collections alone. You need supplies to keep donations in good condition and available for years to come. Here are some low-cost, simple solutions to get you started and the reasons why you and your stakeholders should care to provide a budget for preserving the archives' holdings.

Assess your collection

The first step to taking care of your collection is to assess what you have. What kind of formats does your collection encompass? Books, papers, audiocassettes, CD-ROMs or diskettes? How many of each of these formats are part of your collection? A small inventory will help you not only to assess how many items you have, but it will also help in the next step: to identify what problems your collection may have and what you need to prioritise. Following are the factors that affect the preservation of collections and some solutions for dealing with them.

High temperature and humidity

The ideal temperature for libraries, archives and museums to protect a collection is 60–70°F/16–21°C with a relative humidity between 40–50 per cent (Maher, 1992: 386–7; Ellis, 1999: 52–3). This is recommended to avoid extremes of temperatures that can either dry out paper and make it brittle, or foment the growth of mould. Of the two, I consider mould the worst enemy of archives. Mould is not only dangerous to collections (both paper and non-paper) but it is also hazardous to human beings as many people are allergic to it.

Recommended solutions:

- *Centralised air-conditioning and humidity control* is the most recommended measure to deal with extremes of temperature and humidity. Centralised air-conditioning can be used to lower and stabilise temperatures and centralised humidifiers to lower the relative humidity. The air-conditioning solution, however, has the disadvantage of being very costly – it can run in the thousands of dollars. What to do if you cannot afford central air-conditioning?

- *Stabilise* the temperature of the room where the collections are housed. This is known as the micro-environment approach, where instead of trying to cool off the whole house, library, museum or archives, a room or area is set with the appropriate temperature, humidity and air circulation to protect and maintain the collections. The less the fluctuation in room temperature and humidity, the better the collections will fare. What is recommended?

- *Fans.* Yes, you read it right, fans. They are great providers of air circulation and lower room temperatures and are affordable.

- Also, if you can afford it, buy small portable *humidifiers* as a low-cost alternative to control humidity where you need it most.

Light

Finding the right light for the reading room and other areas where collections will be located is very important. The wrong light can initiate harmful chemical processes, which can accelerate the deterioration of paper. Lack of light, on the other hand, provides a place for pests to hide and eat books at leisure.

Recommended solutions:

- Avoid the use of sunlight or fluorescent bulbs as your main light source. They both have high levels of ultraviolet (UV) light that is harmful to paper.

- Use regular light bulbs with a low wattage. They are better for illumination and for preserving your collections.

- If you must use fluorescent lights, employ UV-filtering sleeves to cover the lights. This will minimise the amount of UV light reaching your collection, but not eliminate it.

Pests

The most common pests in temperate countries are usually cockroaches, silverfish, bookworms, mice and rats. To deal with pests, here is some basic advice – practise good housekeeping. Insects and other types of pests are attracted to food and dust.

Recommended solutions:

- Do not bring food near your collections. Clean areas where food is served, such as kitchens and dining rooms.

- Use the vacuum cleaner often, as this will keep pests away from your collections.

The tidier you keep the archives, the less appetising it will be for pests. If infestation occurs, you need to decide on the best way to eliminate them. The most common way to deal with pests is using pesticides. I do not, however, recommend the use of pesticides because they are highly toxic to humans and animals alike. In addition, some pests may be immune to these toxins.

Recommended solution:

- Re-house materials in acid-free boxes. Take the food (paper) away from the pests.

Acid migration

When papers start turning yellow or brown, that is a sign of high acidity. A classic example is newspaper print. This acidity tends to migrate to all adjacent materials, even if these are not acidic themselves.

Recommended solutions:

- A way to arrest this process is to intersperse acid-free paper between documents.

- If you cannot afford acid-free paper, good quality copier/printer paper is a good alternative.

- If the documents are in danger of fading, or are starting to get too brittle to handle, invest in some good acid-free paper. Most offices have photocopiers. Identify the documents that need urgent attention and make preservation photocopies. Make two sets of copies: a 'master' set copy that can be used to make future reproductions for users and a permanent set to preserve.

Storage conditions

The right storage can help preserve a collection for many years, while bad storage can accelerate chemical reactions that are detrimental to a collection. The key to a good storage area is air circulation. As mentioned in the temperature and humidity section, use fans to ensure good air circulation in any room where you house a collection. Maintaining a constant temperature and humidity will also help to preserve the collection.

How you manage your space is very important. Archives happen all the time; they are just not tidied up to be functional ones! Following these basic recommendations will help you start the process of having this aspect of the archives under control.

Thoughts on digital preservation

The term 'digital preservation' is quite confusing. Some argue that digitising or scanning whole archival collections and placing them on a web server is the 'archival' way of preserving archives. That is incorrect. Scanning pictures or documents does not preserve the original object. If something should happen to the file (e.g. a virus wipes out the web server), the file may disappear but the original object is still in the collection. Digital preservation refers exclusively to the preservation of records 'born' digitally, such as digital pictures, computer files (MS Word, Corel Perfect, MS Access, PDF) including your e-mail, MP3 (sound recordings) files, etc. Electronic records are all around us and they may end up in the archives.

Many factors affect digital preservation. If something happens to an electronic record and you do not have a back-up copy, then it is gone forever. If the technology changes and you do not have the right software or hardware, you may not be able to access the files ever again. Finally, the cost of either digitising or managing electronic records can run in the thousands of dollars. This book cannot go into details on how to preserve digital records but the further reading section does provide suggestions on where to read more about the subject.

If you are just starting your archives, as we were a few years ago, thinking about preserving these records can be quite overwhelming, especially when you barely have enough resources to manage and preserve traditional paper collections. We recommend that you start educating yourself about these problems by visiting some of the many online projects that are trying to find solutions to these issues, in addition to creating standards to preserve and describe these records. Some examples are:

- LIFE: Life Cycle Information for E-Literature: *http://www.ucl.ac.uk/ls/lifeproject/index.shtml*

- Digital Preservation Coalition: *http://www.dpconline.org/graphics/*

- PADI: Preserving Access to Digital Information Gateway: *http://www.nla.gov.au/padi/*

You may not find the answers you seek right away, but at least you will have some ammunition when discussing these issues with your stakeholders. At some point, someone will come to you and demand that you do something about those digital pictures from the latest donors' gala, for example. Take those opportunities to educate your stakeholders about: (1) the difference between access and preservation and (2) the cost of doing either or both types of projects.

Even if you are not managing 'digital archives', you may still have to deal with certain types of electronic objects, such as scanned pictures or documents for your archives' website. If a donor or a department in your institution wants to donate digital pictures, you will need to find a place to store them. A temporary solution is to request computer server space, if available, or even to create a folder on your desktop's local drive. When this type of situation arises, you will want to re-visit your strategic plan, include these issues as the next big challenges for the archives and plan how to attract monetary resources and qualified staff to find a permanent solution. You will need to involve your senior management to receive support and clarification about the evolving function of the archives. Involving your supervisors and other interested stakeholders in these discussions may bring you the support you need to handle such a complicated issue.

Archives 101: arrangement, processing, description and finding aids

Creating a manual that documents how to arrange, process and describe archival collections is a good starting point to set the tone of your archival programme. All of these processes actually happen at the same time. It is both a physical and intellectual process. As you are processing a collection, you are already organising and placing materials in a particular arrangement, which can be either natural or artificial. The collection's description goes hand in hand with its arrangement, and at the end of this process, you pretty much have all the components that you need to create a finding aid. It is important to understand that these processes are guided by archival principles and that they are not done randomly or without reason.

Two archival principles will guide your steps while creating this manual: *provenance* and *original order*. Provenance is a very important principle that cannot be overemphasised in archival practice. The principle of provenance refers to the practice of maintaining the integrity of a collection (created by an organisation, institution or individual) in order to preserve the context of its creation. A related term, *respect des fonds*, reinforces this concept by emphasising that the records created by a particular department or individual should not be mixed with other collections. Contrary to library practices, archival collections are neither broken-up by subject or topic nor intermingled with other collections but retain the creator's original order. The principle of original order refers to the need to keep the records of a collection in the same way they were created and accumulated by its creator. This is done to ensure the integrity, authenticity and reliability of the records found in the archives. Personal papers are the exception to this rule, as they sometimes lack any particular original order. In such cases, the archivist can impose an artificial order to make the collection more accessible to users.

When these two principles (provenance and original order) are applied to the process of archival arrangement and description, we establish intellectual control over the collections in the custody of the archives. The end results are archival records and finding aids that will preserve the information and context of these archives and make them accessible to all users.

Arrangement and description

Why should we bother creating a manual? The main reason for creating the manual is to standardise the process of archival arrangement and description of your archives. This will be apparent when creating archival records and finding aids. The International Council of Archives (ICA) Committee on Descriptive Standards explains:

> The purpose of archival description is to identify and explain the context and content of archival material in order to promote its accessibility. This is achieved by

creating accurate and appropriate representations and by organising them in accordance with predetermined models. Description-related processes may begin at or before records creation and continue throughout the life of the records. These processes make it possible to institute the intellectual controls necessary for reliable, authentic, meaningful and accessible descriptive records to be carried forward through time. (ISAD (G) 1999: 7)[1]

Depending on the location of your archives, you may want to use either a national archival standard (Society of American Archivists) or an international archival standard (International Council on Archives) or a combination of the two if it would better represent your type of archives in the creation of your manual. The idea of using these standards in the manual is to simplify the process of creating archival records and finding aids. Due to the scope of our book, it is not possible to explicate every single rule of archival description. We highly recommended getting the ISAD (G) standard,[2] created by the ICA Archival Description Committee, as a way to get started. It is available via the Web, at no cost. Working with an international standard, in conjunction with your national standard, will help you to create archival records and finding aids that can be shared with a broader, international, audience.

Why is it so important to use standardised archival arrangement and description in your manual? I can offer you three reasons. First, to encourage the creation of uniform descriptions that represent the context and content of a collection or fond. Second, you want to create consistent archival records and finding aids. When more than one person is involved in describing a collection, errors will more readily occur if the rules and examples are not accessible. It is not uncommon to find ten different styles of finding aids in a single repository. This is a problem, especially if you are trying to find information on a particular individual or entity in a collection. A manual will promote good, consistent description, which is essential for continued access to your materials decades after the job is completed. Third, creating records and finding aids that follow a particular standard will help you in the future to transform this information into electronic records that can be added to online union catalogues (more on this in the next section of this chapter).

Whatever standard you choose to use, be consistent. Make the manual simple and make it clear so that anyone with or without archival training can follow it. Adapt or borrow rules from the standards that you have decided to use if it is appropriate, and illustrate a descriptive element clearly. For example, I used part of ISAD (G) rule 3.2.2 Administrative/Biographical History, which has a great explanation of the data I need to record when dealing with persons or families record information or corporate bodies' records information. (For the finding aid template see Appendix R). The closer you keep to the standard, the better the description will be.

Note that the use of any software to create your archival records and finding aids has not been mentioned up to this point. This is a deliberate omission, as it is not feasible to cover all the different software available to create archival records in this book, which is meant to guide and not scare you away from the archival processes! Instead, the basic components are offered, given that in my experience, regardless of which computer program you choose, you will still need to use the same elements to create your finding aids. (See Appendix S for the processing manual).

Processing

Processing is a term borrowed from libraries and commonly used in archives to describe the process of ridding a collection of non-archival material and readying it for arrangement and description. Part of processing is *weeding*. I wrestled with the idea of finding a nicer word than weeding, but I know that honesty is truly the best policy. Weeding is a vital part of processing a collection. To prepare a collection for arrangement, description and preservation, cleaning and discarding materials is needed. What sort of materials should be weeded? Those materials that are superfluous or that do not add to the collection's value.

The word weeding has quite a bad connotation; together with deaccessioning, it is considered by outsiders as something terrible or controversial because of the erroneous assumption that archives are places that keep everything. The best way to avoid weeding a collection is not to accept materials that do not fit the collection development policy in the first place. But that, as you know, is easier said than done.

Do not be afraid to say *no* to a donor, administrator, director, or officer when you are offered materials that you cannot store, process, or are not suitable for the archives. I know this is hard advice to follow, but the attempt needs to be made. You took the time to write your policies and guidelines, so use them to explain why certain materials are not appropriate for the archives. A little education can go a long way, and, you never know, they may accept your explanation. But if your superiors still want you to accept a particular donation or your donor insists on giving you 'all or nothing', go ahead and accept the donation. After doing so, refer to your acquisition guidelines for the weeding rules. Never relinquish the right of the archives to dispose of materials that do not fit the collection. The deed of gift should always include a section on weeding rules and deaccessioning. This way, it is clear to all parties that this is a natural part of the process when preparing a collection's accession. Ask the donor if they would want to be notified in the event of materials being tagged for destruction. This is called the *right of first refusal* and it provides transparency to the donation process. In the long run, the *right of first refusal* will help you avoid misunderstandings and hurt feelings.

Creating standardised finding aids

Finding aids are not difficult to create, but they are time-consuming. A good finding aid will show how the creators of records organised them and what idiosyncratic arrangements were used that reflect the internal structure of an organisation. When dealing with individual personal papers, relationships can be observed between documents and their creators. The historical trajectories of individuals and events demonstrate how the context of creation illuminates the meaning of the content of the materials. Finally, a finding aid is the ultimate access point for users. In order for finding aids to be useful to the widest possible audience it is necessary to use standardised field elements that will allow future users to understand how to find information. The finding aid is the final product of archival description. The information found in finding aids is not arbitrarily gathered but consciously assembled while using archival standards for description.

Finding aids can be divided in two parts: the *front matter* and the *container list*. The front matter contains descriptive, administrative and archival information, which describes the context and content of a collection. The structure and elements in this section will depend on your country's archival description standards. These can be modified and also expanded with the ISAD (G) guidelines. For example, the Online Archives of California use the following structure:

- descriptive summary:
  - title;
  - collection number;
  - extent (boxes amount and linear ft);
  - repository (name of the archives);
  - abstract (brief description of the collection, subject matter, creator and any other relevant information);
  - physical location (where the collection is housed, add a note regarding how to page collection);
  - language (of the materials);
- administrative information:
  - restriction on use and reproduction;
  - restriction on access;
  - provenance/source of acquisition;
  - preferred citation;
- scope and content;
- organisation and arrangement.

The ISAD (G) follows a slightly different order, but ultimately it is composed of the same type of information. Consistency, again, is the key for a good finding aid. Creating a template with the elements that you have decided to use will allow you to maintain the same type of data from finding aid to finding aid and will not only establish but will also maintain the authenticity and reliability of the collections you are managing. (See Appendix T for the finding aid samples).

The second part of a finding aid – and the most intellectual and time-consuming – is the *container list*. This is where you use those levels of arrangement/descriptions that you worked on when you started processing. As mentioned at the beginning of this chapter, all these processes – arrangement, description and processing – are not sequential, but simultaneous. As you clean a collection, you are also seeing the patterns that describe the series and subseries in the finding aid. You are placing the now re-housed materials into their boxes and folders and writing the information down into its computer template or paper finding aid. At the end, after entering all the information about the collection, you should be able to generate a finding aid. If it is possible, you may want to train your personnel to do it in the same manner through the manual. Because this is a repetitive job, mistakes will happen. It is desired that you keep variance between records and finding aids to a minimum. I know this may appear repetitive, but using a template for processing and description will save you time and money from the moment you implement it. You do not want to re-invent the wheel and much less do you want someone after you have left to follow a totally different style because they did not know how to follow the system you established when creating finding aids.

Ultimately, regardless of whether you create a 'traditional' paper finding aid or an electronic version of it, using the same elements from standardised archival description will eventually allow you to take your archives to cyberspace.

Online finding aids and encoded archival description

These days, cyberspace seems to be 'the place to be'. It is quite mind-boggling the way everybody is writing, screaming and yelling that we all need to be there. All the major universities, archives and libraries have some kind of presence on the World Wide Web. Over a thousand trillion bits of information are exchanged on a daily basis. This in and of itself is not a bad thing. Global exchange of information has become very easy to achieve. It is important not to forget that this is not a new phenomenon but actually a normal progression of the automation of libraries and archives. The Library of Congress developed the Machine-Readable Cataloguing Record (MARC) and the MARC 21 formats in the 1960s as a way of creating records that could be read by any computer. In the early 1980s, USMARC was developed and later still a MARC format was created to accommodate archival records, called the USMARC Archival and Manuscripts Control (AMC) format. Most of these developments happened before the Web of today was developed, and computer cards were the way to proceed when it came to exchanging data.

Jumping to the present and skipping a lot of history, encoded archival description (EAD) is quite the thing to do if you have finding aids that you want to make available electronically via the Internet. But what is EAD? Here I must apologise in advance, as there are a lot of jargon and acronyms that need explaining. The Library of Congress (*http://www.loc.gov/ead/*), describes EAD as follows:

> EAD Document Type Definition (DTD) is a standard for encoding archival finding aids using Extensible Markup Language (XML).

EAD is actually a subset of a broader encoding standard called SGML (Standard Generalised Mark-Up Language). HTML (Hypertext Markup Language) and XML are also part of SGML. The history of the development of EAD can be found in other sources (as detailed in the further reading section). However, it is important to understand that the push to use this standard was to improve the accessibility of archival finding aids beyond brick and mortar archives and to reach a global audience through the Web.

EAD finding aids are very versatile. They are expandable and full-text searchable for anyone seeking information. Web links can be added to show cross-reference relations and digital images taken from the original archives can be added as well. As times goes by, more capabilities will be added to this truly adaptable international standard of information exchange.

Should your archives join in and start creating EAD finding aids? The answer is maybe. Your decision to join in this effort of encoding finding aids for the Web will hinge on what resources, experience and time you can dedicate to such a project. The reality is that even if you have the books or attend the workshops, unless you have a good understanding of computer languages, all the information regarding coding EAD sounds like a foreign tongue to most people. Despite this, you may find yourself thrown into creating an online version of your archives and that EAD coding is part of your job description. However, do not despair – there is plenty of help for those of us who are unable to code in EAD.

As this book is an archival primer rather than a specialised treatise on computer language, we are unable to go into the nitty-gritty details of how to learn EAD or how to create an EAD finding aid from scratch. Nevertheless, we are able to refer you to several books that can start you on the path of learning more in-depth details on this topic (see the further reading section for more information). As an archivist, my opinion on the matter is that EAD finding aids are a good thing and serve as a way to make your archives' holdings available to other archives through a union catalogue. But do I believe you need to learn EAD to get your finding aid online? *No.* Here are two low-tech options available to you:

- Add an HTML version of the finding aid to the archives/institution website.

- Use a web template to create an EAD file for your finding aid and submit it to the appropriate union catalogue.

At this point, it is hoped that you have a basic understanding of computer software. You may not have access to the Internet but you are already creating an electronic finding aid. You may be using some type of software for word processing to create your front matter and container list in a document file. That is all that you need to proceed to the next step. I am not an expert HTML programmer and I have used Dreamweaver, an HTML editor, to create my web pages. As it is an HTML editor, it adds the required code for your finding aid. The best advice I can give you is to use tables to place the finding aids' sections, thus keeping the basic structure. It is a rather crude and static way of doing things, but you will have achieved the goal of having the finding aid online.

Regarding the requirement to send EAD finding aids to a national union catalogue, do not panic! There are free tools available to you. For example: in the UK, the Archives Hub website (*http://www.archiveshub.ac.uk/arch/ead.shtml*) offers a free online web template. You can just cut and paste your finding aid and the template will then generate the

EAD code for you. The advantage is that you do not need to code the finding aid tags and the file will be sent to the right union catalogue. Another very useful place is the California Digital Library website, (*http://www.cdlib.org/inside/ projects/oac/toolkit/*). This site offers templates, guidelines and other useful information regarding EAD.

For those new to EAD, all of this information may seem overwhelming. We want you to realise that you are not alone in this part of the process. An EAD finding aid is achievable with a little imagination and resourcefulness.

Notes

1. ISAD (G): general international standard archival description adopted by the Committee on Descriptive Standards. 2nd edn. Stockholm, Sweden, 19–22 September 1999.
2. International Council on Archives, Committee of Descriptive Standards 'Standards and Guidelines'; available at: *http://www .icacds.org.uk/eng/standards.htm* (accessed: 22 December 2005).

Access, archival reference and outreach

Providing access to archival materials and the reference services that allow this access should not be treated as an afterthought, but as an integral part of the process of creating archival policy. Throughout the book, we have discussed many components related to giving access to archival holdings. Chapter 3 outlined the elements needed to create an access policy, Chapter 5 discussed the relationship of donors with the archives, and Chapter 6 explored the issues affecting the preservation of archival collections.

In this chapter, we further discuss how all of these elements combine to fulfil one of the main purposes of archives: to make collections accessible to users without degrading the materials. Your job is to find that fine line between access and preservation. We need to provide and even promote access to collections without harming them, especially when usage statistics are the outcome measure most often used to assign money in the annual budget. There are several factors that you should consider when determining how to provide access to archival collections. You need to balance the needs of the archives to offer equality of access to all authorised users without favouritism or prejudice against the requirements of donors and creators who may require access restrictions to their materials for a specific period of time or for other reasons.

Remember, not all archival collections are equal; access will be determined by restrictions agreed upon with the donors and/or creators, and other restrictions established by the archivist based on solid archival principles, such as appraisal. When developing an archival policy, the relationship with donors and/or creators has a great impact on the way you set up access to archival collections. We must never forget that without donors/creators (and their donations) we would not have an archival programme in the first place. However, their vital feedback must be enriched by your insight. While appraising and describing a collection, you are also identifying possible conditions that may affect the integrity of the collection once it is opened to the public. Setting further restrictions has the purpose of protecting the materials within a collection, as well as ensuring that individuals' privacy and confidentiality are not infringed upon if full accessibility is allowed. Finally, you may want to consider restricting access to materials that are in poor condition and whose handling may accelerate their destruction. To recap, before allowing users physical access to your collections consider these factors:

- Equality of access vs. donor restrictions: There should be no conflict between these two aspects when creating an access policy. Restrictions set by donors/creators should be reasonable. For example, a donor's restrictions should not include a request that the collection never be opened to the public nor prohibit a particular user from using his or her 'collection'. As long as all parties behave ethically, you should be able to offer access to all users and, at the same time, restrict materials in an equitable way.

- Restrictions set by the archivist based on:
  - privacy issues pertaining to creators or other individuals found in the records;

- confidentiality issues relating to creators or other individuals found in the records;
- the condition of the collection (poor or damaged materials).

After creating your access policy, we move now to its implementation: providing physical access to collections through the reading room.

Reading room

Even the smallest of archives should set aside a room or a section of a larger room as a place for users to examine archival collections. If possible, find tables that are big enough for researchers to spread out materials and take notes. Provide pencils to avoid users making notes with pens and possibly damaging the documents. Also have long strips of paper on hand so that users can bookmark specific sections and as a means to steer them away from the temptation of bending or folding documents to mark their place. Set aside space for two sets of shelving areas: one for materials users want to examine, and another for placing binders with your finding aids and any other reference materials (dictionaries, thesauri, indexes, etc.) Even within a modest space, you can create a welcoming environment for your users. A room that is properly lit, quiet and at a comfortable temperature will benefit your users as much as you and your staff. If possible, think creatively and plan to provide a space that is welcoming to all types of users. The aisle between the shelves and the tables should be wide enough for people in wheelchairs, and magnifying glasses should be available for vision-impaired users. It is the small details that can create the best impression.

Locate the reference desk close to the entrance to the reading room. You and your staff should be able to monitor the entire room. This will allow you to supervise the handling of archival materials by the users and also be available to answer any questions they may have. On your desk or on a designated shelf, have on hand any brochures, citation guidelines, policies sheets and rules that explain appropriate behaviour and use of the archives, as well as any forms users may need to request boxes and to make reproductions or photocopies. Develop this literature by using the information you have created through the use of this book. Users should sign any documentation that details access rules and forms, acknowledging that they have read, understood and will abide by the conditions of usage. Here are some suggestions for brochures and sheets you should have at your desk:

- Citation guidelines. List the proper way to cite the materials housed at your archives (see the section on archival citation later in this chapter for examples).

- Donation guidelines.

- Reading room rules. List the proper behaviour expected from users of the reading room (e.g. no food or beverages, no pens, no backpacks or coats, etc.) and explain any rules regarding requesting materials (e.g. one box at a time, last request 30 minutes before closing, etc.)

- Brochures that include a history of the archives, the types of collections housed (highlight the most important), the archives' address, telephone number, URL (if it exists) and your hours of service.

- A summary of your access policy.

- Archives reference records request form (See Appendix U for template).

- Reproduction/photocopying form (should include cost, times when photocopies are made, any conditions regarding the use of the copies, research vs. commercial use, etc.)

Security

In the era of eBay and the Antiques Roadshow, it is more important than ever to think about security in the archives, unless you want your precious documents to end up in auctions, being sold piecemeal. Keep a minimum of two people in the reading room. Believe it or not, the worst thieves of archival materials are users. Your reference desk is the focal point of the reading room. Keep a log of users, and have your visitors check in and out, sign the log and print their name, address, telephone number and affiliation. If possible, set up a space for lockers so that visitors can put away their bags and coats. Restrict the number of boxes that may be requested (e.g. maximum three at a time) and remove folders one at a time. Be vigilant and do not feel ashamed to search their belongings if you see someone has taken something out of a box. Remember that these are standard procedures in many archives around the world, validated by the experiences of many professionals before you.

Setting up your reading room should not be an onerous process. The idea is to create a place where you and your users will feel comfortable and welcome, and will secure the proper access to archival materials for future generations.

Reference services

Is archival reference different from regular reference?

In essence, archival reference is not very different from library reference. Users have information needs and the job of the archivist is to try to meet those needs with the archives' resources. It is at this juncture where you can educate your users on how to use finding aids, inform them of documents that need to be signed (such as reading room rules, waivers, the archives reference checkout tracking form, etc.), types of services offered, and how long it takes to obtain certain services (e.g. paging off-site collections). You can save time by having handouts, brochures and other types of literature available for frequently asked questions. These materials are also useful for outreach. The archives may choose to digitise and post these materials on the archives' website, if there is one. Archives may receive reference questions via telephone or e-mail. Wherever these requests come from, knowing your collections and having good finding aids will help you answer most questions.

The only difference between archival reference and traditional library reference is how you go about accessing your materials. The more complete your finding aids, the easier it will be for you and your users to find the information requested. Seasoned researchers are usually familiar with using archives, but new users may need a brief tutorial on how to use the finding aids. Develop a script that explains the structure of a finding aid (see Appendix R for the finding aids template) and offer tips on the type of information they need to help them identify the materials they need. The most challenging users are those who find your archives on the Web. In the age of Google, Yahoo! and other search engines, these users may expect information to appear in seconds and often have no concept of what archives are and how they work. They may not be interested in a collection but only in a single piece of information, e.g. 'I need photos of old boats. Do you have any?' You can prepare for these kinds of questions by creating facsimiles of materials that you think will be of interest to different types of users, from children and young adults doing school assignments to casual visitors and hobbyists interested in subject-specific topics.

The process is very different from a library search, where everything is organised by call number. But do not worry – the more you do it, the more you will know and be comfortable accessing the collections through the finding aids you have created. Within no time, you *will* know where everything is!

Why is it important to cite properly?

Citing properly allows the reader to know where the information they are reading came from. Information that is properly cited can be traced to where it was received from and, if you ever need to get back to it, you will be able to find it again. Complete and proper citation includes all the elements necessary for this tracking process. In other words, series, box and folder numbers are important. Some collections can be very large, with over 20 numbered boxes and 500 folders. Remind your users that it is always better to cite excessively than insufficiently. It is a sure way to avoid being accused of plagiarism or improperly crediting sources.

Citing archival materials

There are now many online sites that show you how to properly cite, but, unfortunately, most do not show you how to cite archival materials. The few sites that you will find are directed at specific archives, so they either supply you with their preferred citation for their materials or nothing at all. You will have to create your own preferred citation for your archives' materials. At the end of this section you will be given the elements necessary for this. But if you are allowing researchers to use your materials before you are able to create the archives' preferred citation, here are some examples of important elements to consider when citing films, letters, maps, photographs and sound recordings.

Films

- Title;
- director's name (if known);
- producer's name (if known);
- film company (if any);
- date;
- format;
- running time;
- featured performer/s;
- title of collection;
- name of archives;
- depository's location.

An example using the *Chicago Style citation format*:

> *Structure*: Name of Archives. Collection #. Title of Collection. Series Title. Title of Film. Year.

Example: Archives of Ontario. F 10-1-0-4. Mitchell F. Hepburn fonds. Hepburn family sound and moving image material. Gene Autry at Farm [motion picture film]. 1940.[1]

Letters

- Creator's name;
- recipient's name;
- date written;
- title of collection;
- name of archives;
- depository's location.

Letters tend to be cited most commonly. Here are three examples for citing a letter in a collection:

Chicago Style citation format
Structure: Title of Collection. Name of Archives. Depository's Location.
Example: Rinker, Ella V., and Reuben E. Hammon. Papers. Rare Book, Manuscript, and Special Collections Library, Duke University, Durham. (Optional Title of Letter).

MLA Style citation format
Structure: Creator. Title of item. Date. Title of Collection. Name of Archives. Depository's Location.
Example: Miller, Ella. Letter to Ella V. Rinker. Mar. 1865. Ella V. Rinker and Reuben E.

Hammon Papers. Rare Book, Manuscript and Special Collections Lib., Duke U, Durham.[2]

Turabian Style citation format

Structure: Creator. Title of item and date. Title of Collection. Name of Archives. Depository's Location.

Example: Miller, Ella, to Ella V. Rinker, March 1856. Ella V. Rinker and Reuben E. Hammon Papers. Rare Book, Manuscript, and Special Collections Library, Duke University, Durham, North Carolina.[3]

Maps

- Title of map (what does it map);
- year (if available);
- title of collection;
- name of archives;
- depository's location.

For example:

Chicago Style citation format

Structure: Name of Archives. Collection #. Collection's Title. (Optional Title of Map).

Example: Virginia Reid Moore Archives at the Cabrillo Marine Aquarium. Cabrillo Marine Aquarium Map Collection. Palos Verdes Peninsula.

MLA Style citation format (cite as an anonymous book)
Structure: Title of Map. Add the word 'Map' after it. Title of collection. Name of depository.
Example: Palos Verdes Peninsula. Map. Cabrillo Marine Aquarium Map Collection. Virginia Reid Moore Archives at the Cabrillo Marine Aquarium.

Photographs

- Creator (photographer);

- title of photograph (what is photographed);

- year (if available);

- title of collection;

- name of archives;

- depository's location.

For example:

Chicago Style citation format
Structure: Name of Archive. Collection #. Title of Collection. (Optional title).
Example: Archives of Ontario. Series RG 49-33. Ontario Legislative Library print collection.

MLA Style citation format
Structure: Title of Photograph. Name of Archives. Title of Collection. Photographer. Year.
Example: Elizabeth Fry. Archives of Ontario. Series RG 49-33. Ontario Legislative Library print collection. CA. 1850.

Sound recordings

- Featured performer/s;
- title of recording;
- year;
- producer's name (if known);
- format;
- running time;
- title of collection;
- name of archives;
- depository's location.

For example:

> *Chicago Style citation format*
> *Structure*: Name of Archive. Collection's #. Title of Collection. (Optional Title of Sound Recording).
> *Example*: Archives of Ontario. RG 47-27-1. Ontario historical studies series oral history program – political interviews.

> *MLA Style citation format*
> *Structure*: Begin with the name of the person you want to emphasise: the composer, conductor, or performer. For a long work, give the title, underlined, followed by names of pertinent artists (such as performers, readers, or musicians) and the orchestra and conductor (if relevant). End with the manufacturer and the date.

Example: Bizet, Georges. *Carmen*. Perf. Jennifer Laramore, Thomas Moser, Angela Gheorghiu and Samuel Ramey. Bavarian State Orch. and Chorus. Cond. Giuseppe Sinopoli. Warner, 1996.

The previous samples are used to illustrate the essential elements for a given type citation. Although they may appear similar they are not. There are subtle differences in indentation and use of italics need to be noticed to cite correctly.

Creating your own preferred citation

To help you create your archives preferred citation, here are elements you may want to consider to be required in the citation structure:

- creator's name;
- recipient's name;
- date written;
- title of collection;
- name of depository;
- depository's location;
- year;
- format.

For example:

Identification of item, Title of Collection. Name of Depository, Depository location.

Photograph of W. Collection X. Archives Y Depository. Depository of Archives Y at Z Institution.

There are many sources available for you to direct users on how to cite materials in their bibliographies or papers. These are provided in the further reading section.

How to promote your archives

You have created your archives, you have finding aids for each of your collections and the reading room is in place. Now, where are your users? Archives, unlike libraries, are not places that people visit as a matter of course. Most people confuse archives with museums or worse, they think of archives as old buildings full of ancient, dusty boxes. Ultimately, you want to bring users to your archives and educate your community of users on how your archives are relevant to their life. This means that you will need to make time to advertise to your institution, donors and the local community, to let them know what archival resources are available to them.

There are several ways to begin reaching out to your stakeholders. Whether you embark on one or all of the projects suggested in this section is up to you, but you need to start as soon as possible in order to get people to your archives. Otherwise, you just have a room full of boxes. And you did not go through all the trouble of establishing your archives for that, right?

Traditional exhibitions

A traditional exhibition requires some planning and a good selection of materials to showcase a theme. Depending on space, you may want to start small and build up from one success to another. If preservation is an issue, use facsimiles of documents and pictures to avoid accidentally damaging your priceless records. If you cannot afford an exhibit case, use a table. Create posters with information regarding the context of the materials exhibited. Involve your stakeholders in the process. Create a committee to plan an exhibition and pool resources from your committee members. These can be previous donors, members of the community, co-workers and nearby institutions with missions similar to your organisation. Make the exhibition relevant to your stakeholders (e.g. showcase a particular collection and involve either the creators or donors for feedback on what can be added to enhance it). Ask your committee members if they know others who may want to lend materials for the exhibition. Contact these persons and take advantage of the opportunity to educate them on the archives and what you are planning to do. Improvise. You will be amazed by the results. The important thing is that you make the effort and create an exhibition while also involving your stakeholders. For my first archival exhibition, we wanted to commemorate the tenth anniversary of a student hunger strike. We only had a tiny room to set up the exhibition and we did not have display cases, so we borrowed four long tables and set them up in a square to lay out the materials. We created labels to go with the materials, telling the story and explaining what the documents represented. We contacted some of the students who had been involved with the strike and they loaned us photographs of the event. It did not seem like much at first, but in the end we had a nice exhibition and over 200 people came to the opening. People came in and walked around the tables and admired our handiwork. It is not impossible to work with scarce resources; you just need a little creativity and a lot of teamwork from your stakeholders.

Workshops

Another way to reach out to your stakeholders is by offering workshops. Create a list of possible topics that may interest your stakeholders. Some suggestions:

- *Genealogy research tips*: Teach your budding or amateur genealogists how to use your finding aids and other tricks to find those records they need in order to finish their family tree.

- *Neighbourhood history*: Teach your community how to save its history and how the archives can be a place to preserve it.

Talk to your stakeholders and ask them what they would like to see offered by the archives. The key idea is to involve them and make them see how relevant the archives, like libraries, can be to their lives.

Archives' website and virtual exhibitions

For what now seems a long time, archives have found themselves the invisible components of historical preservation when compared with sister institutions such as libraries. This fact is especially pertinent when considering small archives. A way to handle this lack of visibility is by designing your archives 'virtually'. More and more major archives are taking some of their key collections and creating virtual exhibitions or placing their finding aids online. But what if you do not have the resources or the knowledge to create an online exhibit? Start small and see if you can create or find someone to build a simple web page that explains the basics about your archives. You can use the text already created for your brochures and have web pages that highlight the history of your archives, the archival holdings, hours of operation, policies and rules. If you have an e-mail address, include it in the website. Keep records of how many enquiries you receive through this online presence and use those statistics to request more money, supplies, web server space, software and anything else you need to expand your presence. With more resources you can then tackle bigger projects, such as digitisation and scanning projects or creating online exhibitions that mirror the traditional ones. Although discussing how to create a web page or scanning quality images is beyond the scope of this book, we want to encourage you to think big. You can eventually create a website that can showcase and offer to a wide variety of users all the amazing materials housed in your archives. The Internet is here to stay and you need to plan for the future and be ready. Consider taking classes or workshops on web design. Do not be overwhelmed by the jargon or the technology. More important than creating a 'pretty' website is the quality of its content. And for that, you are the expert.

Challenges for the small or non-profit organisation

Multiple users, multiple needs

When thinking about providing access to your archives, you need to think beyond providing finding aids and a well-appointed reading room. Expand your thinking beyond your traditional users, such as historians, genealogists and academic researchers, to include younger users, the disabled, minorities and any other non-traditional users who may have never thought of archives as viable resources.

How do you go about meeting all of these potential user groups' needs? Quite simply, in the best way you can with the resources you have. Case-in-point: the archives where I work now is located on the second floor. As we do not have wheelchair access to the second floor and that is where the reading room is located, how do we serve this special population? We bring down the desired materials to the library reference section so that patrons in wheelchairs can still consult them. Sometimes you need to go out of your way to serve your users.

Just because users do not visit often, it does not mean that they will not want to know about your collections. If your archives are located in an ethnically-diverse community, create materials in multiple languages and reach out to the different ethnic groups. Outside the world of scholarly research, those who use archives are a relatively small group. Considering the pressure to remain relevant in today's multicultural society, it is crucial for you to reach out to your potential users. New users are not an option but an essential element to the success of your archives. In the end, your newest users may also become your future donors.

Notes

1. Archives of Ontario 'Guide to citing archival records'; available at: *http://www.archives.gov.on.ca/english/guides/csg_107_citing.htm* (accessed: 22 December 2005). For further information on this format, see also *The Chicago Manual of Style* (2003).
2. Duke University Libraries 'Citing sources – assembling a list – letter (unpublished)'; available at: *http://www.lib.duke.edu/libguide/cite/letter_unpub.htm* (accessed: 22 December 2005). For further information on this format, see also *http://www.mla.org*. Further information on these formats is available at: *http://www.press.uchicago.edu/Misc/Chicago/cmosfaq/cmosfaq.html*.
3. Hacker, D. 'Humanities: documenting sources – MLA list of works cited'; available at: *http://www.dianahacker.com/resdoc/humanities/list.html* (accessed: 22 December 2005). For further information on this format, see Turabian (1996).

9

Conclusion

We know that we have thrown a lot at you in the past eight chapters. Now we want to reassure you that it is indeed possible to create functional archives without first having to delve into long theoretical and philosophical questions regarding archives and what is archival.

It is our hope that you will get out of this book as much as we have put into it. We strived to provide you with easy ways to set up an archival programme, while letting you know, along the way, that the timeframes are up to you. This is because you are the one who knows exactly what situation you are or will be dealing with, as you begin to create archives to meet the needs of your constituents and institution.

All of the chapters were set up to stand alone, so feel free to jump around. Just read the parts that you need and, eventually, it will become clear how all of the pieces fit together. The point is to facilitate the execution of all the processes required to get underway. For example, Chapter 6 could have been the first chapter, but let us be honest, when you were told 'you are now in charge of the archives', you were not also handed a budget and an interior designer to coordinate the spatial needs of your soon-to-be blossoming archives. In our experiences, we were merely shown the room (or closets) where boxes of materials were kept, followed by: 'You need to organise this and do not expect to get a significant budget or even a budget at all to do so'. As the archivist, your job is to salvage, inventory, execute some preservation measures (*triage* seems a more accurate word), create finding aids, prepare exhibitions and be ready to give tours and assist researchers who may arrive asking for help in finding sources so that they can continue with their research.

We began the book with a chapter that makes you think through the whole process, thus forcing you to evaluate whether you even have an archival collection to start working with. Believe it or not, some people consider paper clippings and other ephemeral items archival simply because someone told them that they were, without ever having checked if the items were in fact special or indeed archival.

With the help of this guide, you are now on your path to getting what you need to start creating your archives. We hope you will find it useful throughout the entire process. Remember, it can take years before you have created your ideal archives, but if you lay the foundation well now, you will only thrive and avoid many setbacks.

After having gone through this book, we trust you see that in time you will have all the pieces in place. For those for whom this book will not be enough, we offer a section of further reading with a more extensive list of books on the theoretical and historical background of the archival sciences. These provide more in-depth information as to why archival practices are the way they are today, as well as the history behind them. Remember that the goal of this book was to be practical and not to bog you down with too much information. As it is, we feel that we managed to get a whole lot of information about archives into this little book.

Appendix A
Collection survey template

Surveyor:				
Collection title:		Creator:		
Date of survey:		Collection number.:		
Type of records by collection	General condition (cleanliness of collection)	Poor condition (preservation measures recommended)	At risk condition (conservation measures required to save information and/or object)	Recommendations (e.g. preservation copies, freezing materials, discarding)
Ephemera (newspaper clippings, flyers, etc.)				
Audiovisual materials (photographs, tapes, film, CDs, etc.)				
Manuscripts (letters, notes, notebooks, holograph manuscripts)				
Printed materials (books, magazines, reports, etc.)				
Other				

Suggestions by condition

General condition	Poor condition	At-risk condition
Folded or rolled documents	Highly acidic/brittle	Crumbling items
Metal fasteners/clips/ staplers	Water marks	Mould
Dead silverfish/ cockroaches	Cockroach eggs	Live pest(s) (silverfish/ cockroaches)
Glue or tape on documents/photographs	Soiled documents and/or tapes	Water damage (wet materials)
Acidic boxes/folders	Scratches on CDs	Vinegar syndrome (vinegary smell on film canisters or boxes)

Appendix B
Inventory worksheet template

Department/Office: _____

Person Completing Inventory: _____

Date: _____

Location	Room	Area	Storage Equipment	Volume	Years	Brief Title

Based on Maher (1992) *The Management of College and University Archives* template form in Appendix 5.

Appendix C
Mission statement samples

Iowa State University Special Collections Department Archives of Women in Science and Engineering

The Archives of Women in Science and Engineering seeks to preserve the historical heritage of American women in science and engineering. To do this, the Archives solicits, collects, arranges, and describes the personal papers of women scientists and engineers as well as the records of national and regional women's organizations in these fields.

The Archives will also serve as a local, regional, national, and international resource for information on women in science and engineering, with a particular emphasis on K-12 and college level students.

Archives of the Pentecostal Assemblies of Canada

The Archives of the Pentecostal Assemblies of Canada exists to collect, preserve, and provide access to materials and records related to the history and activities of the PAOC for the purpose of administrative support and historical research.

Oakland Public Library

The Oakland Public Library informs, inspires, and delights our diverse community as a resource for information, knowledge, and artistic and literary expression, providing the best in traditional services, new technologies, and innovative programs.

University of California at Berkeley Library

UC Berkeley Library connects students and scholars to the world of information and ideas. With a daily commitment to excellence and innovation, we select and create, organize and protect, provide and teach access to resources that are relevant to our campus programs and pursuits.

New York State Archives

The New York State Archives leads efforts, on behalf of all New Yorkers, to manage, preserve, ensure open access to, and promote the wide use of records that support information needs and document the history, governments, events, and peoples of our State. We strive for comprehensive, equitable, and accessible documentation of our present, past and future through innovative partnerships and state-of-the-art approaches.

Appendix D
Vision statement samples

The University of California libraries

Individually and collectively, the University of California libraries provide access to the world's knowledge for the UC campuses and the communities they serve. In so doing, they directly support UC's missions of teaching, research, and public service.

New York State Archives

The New York State Archives provides unparalleled services that build, maintain, and provide access to New York's records to sustain a free, open, and democratic society and to support the cultural and intellectual life of all New Yorkers. We relentlessly pursue excellence in all our endeavors.

Milwaukee Public Library

The Milwaukee Public Library is every person's gateway to an expanding world of information. Providing the best in library service, we guide Milwaukeeans in their pursuit of knowledge, enjoyment, and life-long learning, ultimately enriching lives and our community as a whole.

The Elvehjem Museum of Art

The Elvehjem Museum of Art will be a leader among university art museums. Supported by the resources of the Kohler Art Library, it will be a dynamic centre for research, education, and experimentation in the visual arts.

Duke University Medical Center Library & Archives: online vision

To be a leading archival repository by:

- Providing departments, centers, programs, and offices with innovative records management services,
- Delivering high quality, innovative responses to administrative and research requests for DUMC/DUHS information, and
- Developing resources and programs to pro-actively document the history and development of the DUMC/DUHS.

Appendix E
Strategic plan: SWOT analysis layout sample

Strengths:	Weaknesses:
Opportunities:	Threats:

Based on class notes from library management class at UCLA, Spring 2000, and Swinton, *How To Do A SWOT Analysis: Strategic Planning Made Easy* *(http://www.trans4mind.com/counterpoint/swinton3.shtml).*

Appendix F
Strategic plan outline

Title: Strategic Plan of Archives X

Mission:

Vision:

Issues the archives must address to achieve the mission:

- Internal influences:
- External influences:

Goals to achieve in the next year:
Goal 1:

- Objective:
- Objective:
- Objective:

Goal 2:

- Objective:
- Objective:

Goal 3:

- Objectives:

Goals to achieve in the next three years: (optional)

Goals to achieve in the next five years: (optional)

Goals to achieve in the next ten years: (optional)

Assessment: Progress towards attaining goals will be checked through quarterly evaluations and assessment of the objectives completed up to that point.

January_____   April_____

July_____   October_____

Appendix G
Archives policy template

A. Vision statement.

B. Core mission statement.

C. Goals.

D. Objectives.

E. Collection policy:

(a) Purpose;

(b) User community (list current and future users);

(c) Scope of coverage (list subject areas, geographical area, languages, chronological limits, date of publication type of materials, exclusions);

(d) Cooperative collection development (any policies/ agreements with other departments that share the collection);

(e) Statements concerning resource sharing (policies/ agreements with other similar institutions);

(f) Summary of acquisition/donation policy;

(g) Summary of access policy;

(h) Summary of deaccessioning policy;

(i) Collections housed in archives (list location of collections if placed in more than one room or building);

(j) Procedures for reviewing collection development policy (summarise procedures for revision stated in strategic planning document).

F. Acquisition/donation policy.

G. Access policy.

H. Deaccessioning policy.

I. Organisational chart.

Appendix H
Acquisition/donation policy template

Acquisition/donation policy

A. Mission of archives.

B. Statement of responsibility.

C. Evaluation criteria (list what factors are used to accept or reject donations).

D. What to donate (offer examples).

E. Donation protocol.

F. Acquisition guidelines.

G. Transfer of materials (deed of gift).

H. Restrictions.

I. Copyrights.

J. Monetary appraisal.

K. Care of collection.

L. Purchases (archives' position).

Appendix I
Access policy template

Access policy

A. Type of services (e.g. by appointment, e-mail, telephone).

B. Reading room rules.

C. Photocopy services (e.g. copyright permission forms, releases).

D. Authorised users (level of access).

E. Restrictions on access.

F. Hours of operation.

G. Exclusions (e.g. unprocessed materials).

H. Preferred citation.

Appendix J
Deaccessioning action plan: sample scenarios

Material in storage is found to be infected with mould

- Archivist or authorised staff is informed.
- After revising the material for damage:

  A. start conservation measure, or

  B. discard materials.

If (B), leave documentation regarding the deaccessioning action in the original box and in the collections file.

A donor's heir disputes the right of the archives to an original donor gift

- Archivist or authorised staff research collection file for deed of gift.
- After researching, it is found that there is no deed of gift.
- Archivist informs immediate supervisor of situation

  A. the institution fights the heir legally, or

  B. the collection is returned to the heir.

If (B), leave documentation regarding the deaccessioning action in the original box and in the collections file.

Note: You can create more than one scenario to cover all possible actions. In addition, if a situation arises that you did not anticipate, use this opportunity to add the new scenario to your action plan.

Appendix K
Archive deaccessioning policy sample

A. Reasons for this policy – To remove items of little relevance or in poor condition, space problems, and/or the cost of maintenance or storage. The practice of deaccessioning is best avoided by attending to the accepted collection development policy.

   (a) Deaccessioning: Process to remove permanently a collection/item/object to refine a collection. Also known as weeding, deselection, and reappraisal.

B. Criteria for deaccessioning:

   (a) Physical condition

      i. Damage to the extent that the item is no longer usable.

      ii. Item/collection has deteriorated beyond a reasonable means of conservation or in deteriorating has lost its usefulness.

   (b) Collection development and/or management

      i. No evidence of clear legal title.

      ii. Unnecessary multiple copies (usually exceeding two).

      iii. The authenticity, attribution, or genuineness of the item is determined to be false or fraudulent.

      iv. The possession of the object is determined to be illegitimate.

      v. Lack of consistency with collection development policies, i.e. erroneous inclusion in the collection.

C. Use a deaccessioning action plan to determine the appropriate action.

D. After deaccessioning:

      i. A copy of the documentation pertaining to the item/collection will be retained in the collection archives (files).

Appendix L
Deaccessioning policy template

Deaccessioning policy

A. Statement of responsibility (Who implements the policy, e.g. archivist).

B. Definition.

C. Rationale (explain in lay terms why materials may be deaccessioned – this is one of the most sensitive topics when dealing with donors).

D. Guidelines:

   (a) Physical condition (brittleness, mould, water damage).

   (b) Collection development and/or institutional decision:

   i. unclear legal title or ownership;

   ii. multiple copies;

   iii. issues of accuracy, authority or authenticity;

   iv. unfitness to current or revised collection policy;

   v. right of first refusal (always try to contact donor to inform of deaccessioning decision).

E. Procedure (establish a decision tree that clearly defines when and how materials will be discarded):

(a) List forms that need to be completed to keep a record of materials removed from archives.

(b) List actions and location where materials will be disposed of.

(c) List individuals and departments that need to be notified of final disposition of materials.

Appendix M
Prospective donor's form template

Prospective Donor Name: _____   _____
                                    Last   First

Prospective Donor Address: _____

_____

Telephone number: _____

Type of Contact:
☐ Telephone   ☐ Visit to archives   ☐ Visit to donor's home

Date: _____

Type of Collection:
☐ Personal Papers   ☐ Organisational Papers

Type of Materials:
☐ Ephemera   ☐ Memorabilia
☐ Papers/Manuscripts   ☐ Photographs
☐ Audiotapes   ☐ Other media

Comments: _____

_____

_____

Follow-up (Add more sheets as necessary):

Date: _____

Comments: _____

Date: _____

Comments: _____

Final Decision:
☐ Accept Collection   ☐ Reject Collection

Recommendations: _____

Appendix N
Appraisal survey template

Surveyor:			Subject of collection:			
Date:			Donor:			
Appraisal survey	Very Clear/ Good (5)	Clear/ Good (4)	Moderately Clear/ Good (3)	Somewhat Clear/ Good (2)	Unclear/ Poor (1)	Total
Provenance						
Copyrights						
Ownership						
Reliability of information						
Relevance to archives						
Administrative value (if dealing with organisational materials)						
Evidential value						
Informational value						
Intrinsic/ historical value						
Monetary value						
					Total Points	

Scale:
50–41   Must acquire
40–31   Acquire
30–21   Acquire with reservation
20–10   Do not acquire

Appendix O
Donor registry template

Donor Registry

Name of donor	Contact address	Phone number	Heir(s) or estate executor (if applicable)	Signed deed of gift (yes/no)	Date of signed deed	Collection number	Extent (in linear ft.)

Appendix P
Sample of deed of gift with transfer of copyright

Deed of gift with transfer of copyright and some restrictions

Note: Consult your legal department or a lawyer to verify that your forms are legally binding.

I, [**Name of Donor**], of [**Address**], do hereby make a gift of the material specified below to the [**Name of your archives/institution**] and its successor organisations.

Being the sole owner of the material, I give this material (and any additional materials which I may add to it at a later date) unencumbered to the [**Name of the archives**] and do declare that I made this gift of my own free will and without influence.

Any copyright such that I may possess in this material or of any other property in custody of [**Name of archives**] are hereby assigned to the [**Name of archives**].

The material specified bellow shall be available to members of the public for use from [**Date of the deed**] with the exception of the items asterisked below which shall be restricted from public used until *1 January* [**Insert year**].

I have the *right of first refusal* for items not retained by the [**Name of archives**].

Materials donated:

- ■ (e.g.) Pre- and post-manuscripts, 1910–1965 (10 boxes)
- * Diaries of [**Name of donor**], 1970–1975 (2 boxes)
- ■ Photograph albums (various dates) 12 albums

In full accord with the provisions of this deed of gift, I hereunto set my hand.

_____   Date _____
(Donor)

Witness signature _____ (if applicable)

On behalf of [**Name of archives**], I, [**Name of authorised official**], [**Title**], accept this gift

_____   Date _____

Source: Schwirtlich and Reed (1999: 152).

Appendix Q
Sample of deed of gift without transfer of copyright

Deed of gift without copyright transfer

Note: Consult your legal department or a lawyer to verify that your forms are legally binding.

I, [**Name of Donor**], of [**Address**], do hereby make a gift of the material specified below to the [**Name of your archives/institution**] and its successor organisations.

Being the sole owner of the material, I gift this material (and any additional materials which I may add to it at a later date) unencumbered to the [**Name of the archives**] and do declare that I made this gift of my own free will and without influence.

I retain any copyrights to the material such that I may possess in this donation or in any other property in custody of [**Name of archives**].

The material specified below shall be available to members of the public for use from [**Date of the deed**].

I have the *right of first refusal* for items not retained by the [**Name of archives**].

Materials donated:

- (e.g.) Pre- and post-manuscripts, 1912–1999 (15 boxes)
- Diaries of [**Name of donor**], 1966–1975 (7 boxes)
- Photograph albums (various dates) 12 albums

In full accord with the provisions of this deed of gift, I hereunto set my hand.

_____   Date _____
(Donor)

Witness signature _____ (if applicable)

On behalf of [**Name of archives**], I, [**Name of authorised official**], [**Title**], accept this gift

_____   Date _____

Source: Schwirtlich and Reed (1999: 152). Further adapted to create a deed of gift without transfer of copyright.

Appendix R
Finding aid template

Note: This is just a sample and does not represent all the elements required in a finding aid.

The following elements must be recorded while processing the collection to create the collection's finding aid.

Front matter

If using ISAD (G) standard:

Reference code: U.S. CMA 11 [ISO 3166 Codes for the representation of names of countries; Repository Code, Local Code/Collection number]

Title: Provide either a formal title or a concise supplied title for the collection.

For example:

Cabrillo Marine Aquarium organisational records (formal title)

Luke Smith Personal Papers 1913–2005 (title supplied by archivist)

Date(s): The date or dates of the collection described. Dates can be a single date or a range of dates.

For example:

January 1998

1935–2005

[c.1977]–2000

1955–1965 (dates of creation of the material)

Level of description: Specify the level of arrangement used to describe the collections.

For example:

Collection/fond

Subfond

Series

Subseries

Folder/file

Item

Extent of the unit of description: Describe the extent of the collection. You can use the following measures:

For example:

100 linear feet (200 document boxes)

345 VHS tapes

1 folder, containing 12 items

Name of creator(s): Identify the creator(s) of the collection; organisation(s) or individual(s).

For example:

Olguin, John (1901–)

Great Pacific Cruiser Company (U.S.)

Department of Defense

Administrative/biographical history: Brief description of the collection, subject matter, creator, and any other relevant information.

For example:

- For persons or families, record information such as full names and titles, dates of birth and death, place of birth, successive places of domicile, activities, occupation or offices, original and any other names, significant accomplishments, and place of death.

- For corporate bodies, record information such as the official name, the dates of existence, enabling legislation, functions, purpose and development of the body, its administrative hierarchy, and earlier, variant or successive names.

Provenance/source of acquisition: Document how the collection was obtained. Include full name of donor and/or full name of creator and date of acquisition. If donor is unknown, make a note in this section.

For example:

Gift of the Edgar Bowers estate, 2002.

Scope and content: Give a summary of the scope (such as time periods, geography) and content, (such as documentary forms, subject matter, administrative processes) of the unit of description, appropriate to the level of description.

Organisation and arrangement/system of arrangement: Specify the internal structure, order and/or the system of classification of the unit of description. Note how these have been treated by the archivist.

For example:

> The original order of the collection/fonds has been maintained and arranged into ten (10) series, which reflect the major activities of the creator over a period of thirty (30) years.

> The collection was arranged chronologically by year, alphabetically by name or acronym of office at the series level.

> The collection was arranged in the following series and subseries:

> 1) Manuscripts
>> a) Manuscripts by Edgar Bowers
>> b) Manuscripts by other authors

Archivist notes: Record notes on sources consulted in preparing the description and who prepared it.
For example:

> The collection was originally processed by Marisol Ramos-Lum in 2002. In preparation for the Department's 2003 Bowers conference and exhibit, Kevin Durkin and Octavio Olvera completed additional processing in the correspondence and manuscripts series. Royce Dieckmann reprocessed the collection in the summer of 2005 and created a finding aid for the collection with the assistance of Laurel McPhee; machine-readable finding aid created by Caroline Cubé; online material edited by Josh Fiala, Caroline Cubé, Laurel McPhee, and Amy Shung-Gee Wong. UCLA Library, Department of Special Collections.

> Processed by: Lydia Lucas, May 1996; Lara Friedman-Shedlov, May 1999.

Container list

This is the structure to be followed when creating the container list:

- Series title
- Box number
- Folder/file number
- Folder/file title
- Item number (if applicable)

For example:

Series 1: Correspondence, 1886–2001. 4 boxes.

This series includes letters to and by Edgar Bowers, arranged alphabetically by the surname of the correspondent. Letters written by Edgar Bowers to various people are arranged under his name, followed alphabetically by the name of the recipient.

[Box 1]

[Folder 1]

Alexander, John. 1995. 2 items.

Letter from John Alexander to Edgar Bowers regarding gift of book Chaco Body, and a note from Vincent Price to Judith Anderson originally enclosed in the book.

Appendix S
Processing manual sample

Note: This is just a sample and does not represent all the elements required in a processing manual.

Purpose of manual: These are the official guidelines to process any collection acquired by the [place name] archives and to create a collection's finding aid. This manual uses the [insert title of standard] archival standard for describing titles, creators' names, dates and any other archival description elements.

Types of collections acquired by archives:

- *Personal papers*: The accumulated materials of a family or individual.

- *Organisational archives*: Inactive records from a corporate organisation

- *Artificial collections*: Collections put together by a second party that is not the creator of the records.

Data entry protocol: Assign an accession number and collection number. Use number approved by the archivist or authorised personnel. Create a new file using the MS Access collection template [or the appropriate software template]. See the finding aid section for instructions and examples on how to input each field/element into template.

Processing guidelines:

- Remove metal clips and staples.

- Remove letters from envelopes and flatten them.

- If you find multiple copies of the same document, retain only three copies. Replace acidic folders with acid-free ones if available.

- Place photographic materials (prints, negatives) inside non-reactive plastic or acid-free sleeves or envelopes, if available.

- If working with acidic materials such as newspaper print, intersperse acid-free paper to arrest acid transfer.

Elements for labels: All labels should include the following information:

- Left side corner:
    - title of folder;
    - collection number;
    - box number, file/folder number.
- Right side corner:
    - series title;
    - subseries title (if applicable).

Use label template and be sure to use Times New Roman font at 9 points.

Appendix T
Finding aid samples

Short finding aid sample

(No series arrangement was necessary as this collection is composed of three boxes). This finding aid is available at Online Archives of California (*http://www.oac.cdlib.org*).

Title: Hunger Strike for Chicano Studies Department Papers 1993.

Processor Name: Processed by Marisol Ramos-Lum.

Institution Name: Chicano Studies Research Center, UCLA.

Institution address: UCLA, Chicano Studies Research Center Library 144 Haines Hall, Box 951544, Los Angeles, CA 90095-1544. Phone: (310) 206-6052; Fax: (310) 206-1784; URL: *http://www.chicano.ucla.edu/*
Copyright notice: ©2005 The Regents of the University of California. All rights reserved.

Descriptive summary

Title: Hunger Strike for Chicano Studies Department Papers, 1993.

Collection number: 1

Creator: Movimiento Estudiantil Chicano de Aztlan (MEChA) 1993.

Extent: 1.5 linear ft. [3 boxes].

Repository: University of California, Los Angeles. Library. Chicano Studies Research Center, UCLA Los Angeles, California 90095-1490.

Abstract: This collection consists of flyers, memos, notes, form letters, faxes, and photographs that document the events that occurred during the summer of 1993 when six students and one professor began a hunger strike to protest the decision of Chancellor Charles R. Young to close the Chicano Studies Program at the University of California, Los Angeles. **Please note that accents have been eliminated in order to accommodate and facilitate the use of all types of web browsers. Researchers who would like to indicate errors of fact or omissions in this finding aid may contact the archivist at *archivist@chicano.ucla.edu*.

Physical location: This collection is currently stored off-site at UCLA's Southern Regional Library Facility (SRLF). Collection materials are in English and Spanish.

Access: Access is available by appointment for UCLA student and faculty researchers as well as independent researchers. To view the collection or any part of it, please contact the archivist at *archivist@chicano.ucla.edu* or the librarian at *yretter@chicano.ucla.edu*.

Publication rights: Publication rights are available to students and faculty researchers at UCLA. All others by permission only. Copyright has not been assigned to the Chicano Studies Research Center. All requests for permission to publish or quote from manuscripts must be submitted in writing to the Archivist at the Chicano Studies

Research Center Library. Permission for publication is given on behalf of the UCLA Chicano Studies Research Center as the owner of the physical items and is not intended to include or imply permission of the copyright holder, which must also be obtained.

Preferred citation: [Identification of item], Hunger Strike for Chicano Studies Department Papers, 1, Chicano Studies Research Center, UCLA, University of California, Los Angeles.

Acquisition information: Movimiento Estudiantil Chicano de Aztlan (MEChA) ca. 1993.

Historical background

In the spring of 1993, after several attempts by faculty and students at the University of California, Los Angeles to change the standing of the Chicano Studies Program from an interdisciplinary program to a department, Chancellor Charles E. Young announced that the Program would not receive departmental status. The date was April 28th, 1993, the eve of Cesar Chavez's funeral.

This decision ignited the passion and activism of many students and set in motion a sit-in demonstration by the Conscious Students of Color over the welfare of the Chicano Studies Library, budget cuts, and the Chicana/o Studies Program and other Ethnic Programs at UCLA. Around 200 hundred students walked across the Westwood campus to the Faculty Center on campus to protest the Chancellor's decision. The protest turned violent after Los Angeles Police Department (LAPD) and University of California Police Department (UCPD) officers appeared in riot gear at the Faculty Center. As a result, 99 students were arrested and

UCLA pressed charges against the students for vandalising the premises.

The most dramatic demonstration and the focus of this archival collection was the 1993 hunger strike. Eight students and one UCLA professor decided to protest what they considered an injustice on the part of UCLA Administration, represented by Chancellor Charles R. Young, through a fast to emphasise their demands. The hunger strikers were: Juan Arturo Diaz Lopez, Marcos Aguilar, Balvina Collazo, Maria M. Lara, Arturo Paztel Mireles Resendi, Cindi Montanez, Joaquin Manual Ochoa, and Professor Jorge R. Mancillas.

At the end of the hunger strike a compromise was achieved between the hunger strikers and the UCLA administration. As a result, the Cesar Chavez Center for Interdisciplinary Instruction in Chicana and Chicano Studies was created.

Sources

Cesar Chavez Center website at *http://www.sscnet.ucla.edu/ YPC/conference/90sBackground.htm.*

Rhoads, Robert A. Immigrants in Our Own Land: The Chicano Studies Movement at UCLA. In Freedom's Web: Student Activism in an Age of Cultural Diversity, pp. 61–94. Baltimore: Johns Hopkins Press, 1998.

Scope and content

Scope: This collection documents the events that occurred during the summer of 1993, when six students and one professor went on a hunger strike to protest the decision of Chancellor Charles R. Young to close the Chicano Studies Program at the University of California, Los Angeles.

Content: The collection consists of letters of support, flyers, faxes, notes from meetings, memos from the UCLA administration, and photographs.

The collection is organised into the following series:

- faxes;
- signatures of support;
- form letters;
- Cesar Chavez Center creation.

Indexing terms: The following terms have been used to index the description of this collection in the library's online public access catalogue.

Subjects:

- Chancellor Charles R. Young;
- Chicano studies UCLA;
- hunger strike;
- UCLA 1993.

Container list

[Box 1] [Folder 1]

Collection title: THE 1993 HUNGER STRIKE FOR A CHICANO STUDIES DEPARTMENT AT UCLA

Folder title: Faxes Inviting Support for the Hunger Strike. May 1993.

Folder content description: Papers. Fax cover letters sent to politicians in California by students involved in organising the hunger strike.

[Box 2] [Folder 1]

Collection title: THE 1993 HUNGER STRIKE FOR A CHICANO STUDIES DEPARTMENT AT UCLA

Folder title: Form Letters. May 1993. Papers.

Folder content description: Signed form letters in support of the hunger strike.

[Box 3] [Folder 1]

Collection title: THE 1993 HUNGER STRIKE FOR A CHICANO STUDIES DEPARTMENT AT UCLA

Folder Title: Cesar Chavez Center Proposal Papers. Jan–June 1993. Papers.

Folder content description: Two packages of photocopied papers outlining the logistics of creating the Cesar Chavez Center.

Long finding aid sample

(This aid illustrates a series and its complexity in the organisation and arrangement section as well as in the container list. This collection is composed of 18 boxes, 1 shoebox, and 1 oversize box). This finding aid is available at Online Archives of California (*http://www.oac.cdlib.org*).

Finding aid title: Bowers (Edgar) Papers

Processor(s) name(s) and related personnel involved in creating finding aid: The collection was originally processed by Marisol Ramos-Lum in 2002. In preparation for the Department's 2003 Bowers conference and exhibit, Kevin Durkin and Octavio Olvera completed additional processing in the correspondence and manuscripts series. Royce Dieckmann reprocessed the collection in the summer of 2005 and created a finding aid for the collection with the assistance of Laurel McPhee; machine-readable finding aid created by Caroline Cubé; online material edited by Josh Fiala, Caroline Cubé, Laurel McPhee, and Amy Shung-Gee Wong.

Institution name: UCLA Library, Department of Special Collections.

Institution address: Manuscripts Division, Room A1713, Charles E. Young Research Library, Box 951575, Los Angeles, CA 90095-1575. E-mail: *spec-coll@library .ucla.edu*; URL: *http://www.library.ucla.edu/libraries/ special/scweb/*.

Copyright notice: ©2002 The Regents of the University of California. All rights reserved.

Descriptive summary

Title: Edgar Bowers Papers, 1868–2003, (bulk 1920–2000).

Collection number: 565.

Creator: Bowers, Edgar, 1924–2000.

Extent: 18 boxes (9 linear ft.). 1 shoebox (0.5 linear ft.). 1 oversize box.

Repository: University of California, Los Angeles. Library, Department of Special Collections, Los Angeles, California 90095-1575.

Abstract: The Edgar Bowers papers consist of the poet's original correspondence, manuscripts, personal papers, photographs, recordings, and publications that document Bowers' family life, personal history, and development as a poet and scholar.

Physical location: Stored off-site at SRLF. Advance notice is required for access to the collection. Please contact the UCLA Library, Department of Special Collections Reference Desk for paging information.

Administrative information

Restrictions on access: Collection stored off-site at SRLF: Advance notice required for access.

Restrictions on use and reproduction: Property rights to the physical object belong to the UCLA Library, Department of Special Collections. Literary rights, including copyright, are retained by the creators and their heirs. It is the responsibility of the researcher to determine who holds the copyright and pursue the copyright owner or his or her heir for permission to publish where The UC Regents does not hold the copyright.

Provenance/source of acquisition:

- Gift of the Edgar Bowers estate, 2002.
- Gift of Joshua Odell, 2002.

Preferred citation: [Identification of item], Edgar Bowers Papers (Collection 565). Department of Special Collections, Charles E. Young Research Library, University of California, Los Angeles.

Biography: Edgar Bowers was born in Rome, Georgia in 1924. He began writing poetry at a young age, and had published poems in newspapers by the time he was 13 years old. He entered the University of North Carolina in 1942, but his studies were interrupted by World War II. As part of his training, he entered the Army Specialised Training program at Princeton University, where he met a number of sophisticated young men who furthered his commitment to the arts. He served in Bavaria with the counterintelligence corps of the Army's 101st Airborne Division, and was stationed at Berchtesgaden as part of the 'de-Nazification' programme of the US occupation force.

After his discharge in 1946, he completed his undergraduate studies at UNC, and moved to Stanford in 1947 to pursue his master's degree and doctorate. Under the guidance of poet and critic Yvor Winters, he wrote his dissertation on the poetry of T. Sturge Moore, and further developed his poetic sensibilities. He taught at Duke University, Harpur College and, from 1958 until his retirement in 1991, at the University of California, Santa Barbara, where he specialised in English Renaissance and modern poetry. He died in San Francisco in 2000.

Scope and content

The collection consists of Edgar Bowers' original correspondence, manuscripts, personal papers, photographs, recordings, and publications that document Bowers' family life, personal history, and development as a poet and scholar. Of particular interest are letters written during the period between World War II and his graduate studies at Stanford in the 1950s, including letters from Yvor Winters, Robert Lowell, and many other peers and colleagues. The manuscript series includes a significant collection of Bowers' poems, often in variant forms, including unpublished and uncollected works. Other series include manuscripts by other poets edited by Bowers, video and audio recordings of Bowers' readings, journal and little magazine publications, and an extensive assortment of correspondence and documents concerning the Anderson and Bowers families.

Organisation and arrangement

Arranged in the following series:

- Correspondence, 1886–2001 (4 boxes).
- Manuscripts, ca. 1900–2000 (6.5 boxes), Subseries A–C as follows:
- Manuscripts by Edgar Bowers, 1937–2000.
- Notebooks and course materials, ca. 1970–1999.
- Manuscripts by other authors, ca. 1900–1999.
- Miscellaneous, 1868–1999 (2.5 boxes).
- Photographs, ca. 1900–1999 (1 box).
- Cassettes and compact disks, 1966–2000 (1 box).
- Publications and printed materials, 1921–2003 (4 boxes).

Indexing terms

The following terms have been used to index the description of this collection in the library's online public access catalogue.

- Bowers, Edgar – Archives.
- Poets, American – Archives.
- Poetry, Modern – 20th century – Archival resources.

Container list

Series title: Series 1: Correspondence, 1886–2001.

Amount of boxes: 4 boxes.

Series description: This series includes letters to and by Edgar Bowers, arranged alphabetically by the surname of the correspondent. Letters written by Edgar Bowers to various people are arranged under his name, followed alphabetically by the name of the recipient.

[Box 1] [Folder 1]

Folder title: Alexander, John. 1995. *Amount of items*: 2 items.

Folder content description: Letter from John Alexander to Edgar Bowers regarding gift of book Chaco Body, and a note from Vincent Price to Judith Anderson originally enclosed in the book.

Series title: Series 2: Manuscripts, ca. 1900–2000. *Amount of boxes*: 6.5 boxes.

Series description: Arranged in the following Subseries: 2A, Manuscripts by Edgar Bowers, 1937–2000; 2B, Notebooks and course materials, ca. 1970–1999; 2C, Manuscripts by other authors, ca. 1900–1999.

Subseries title: Subseries 2A: Manuscripts by Edgar Bowers, 1937–2000.

Subseries description: Assorted loose leaf manuscripts and annotated proofs. Poetry manuscripts are arranged alphabetically by the given title on manuscript itself; if untitled, by the first line; or if it was published as part of a collection, the publication title.

[Box 5] [Folder 1]

Folder Title: Diaries – Europe trip, 1966, and Italy trip, 1999. 1966, 1999. *Amount of items*: 2 items.

Folder Content Description: Small brown ring binder used as a diary by Bowers during his trip to Greece, France, and Italy in 1966. (Note: A number of holograph poems appear to have been removed from this binder). Spiral bound notebook used as a diary during his trip to Italy in 1999.

Appendix U
Archives reference records request form template

Archives reference checkout tracking	
Name	Date
Address	
Status (check one)	Purpose (check one)
– Faculty	– Dissertation/thesis
– Graduate student	– Course paper/class
– Undergraduate	– Research for publication
– Administrative staff	– Administration
– Other university	– Personal
– Alumni	
– Public	
Subject of study	
Records used (for staff use only)	

Based on Maher (1992) *The Management of College and University Archives* template form in Appendix 5.

Glossary

The purpose of this glossary is to provide definitions and usages of the archival terms employed in this book. The terms supplied in this glossary come from two main sources: the *Dictionary for Library and Information Science* by Joan M. Reitz (2004) and its web version, the *Online Dictionary for Library and Information Science* (*http://lu.com/odlis/*), and *Keeping Archives*, edited by Judith Ellis (1993). We chose these two sources because they offered the most appropriate and easy to read definitions. When a term was not available in either of these sources or was too complex for people outside the archival field, we simplified or created our own definitions. Some tips for using the glossary:

- multiple meanings for a term are listed using numbers;
- when a term is both a noun and a verb it is listed as follows: (*noun*), (*verb*);
- 'see' is used to indicate the preferred similar term;
- 'see also' directs readers to related terms.

Access: The granting of permission to use the reference facilities of an archival programme to users. Access to archives may be restricted or withheld to prevent physical damage to original records or to protect confidential information. See also *Access policy*.

Access policy: A formal written statement issued by the person(s) or body responsible for managing archives or special collections, specifying which materials are available for access and by whom, including any conditions or restrictions on use, usually posted or distributed by some method to users.

Acquisition: The process of selecting and receiving materials for archival collections by donation, gift or exchange.

Administrative value: The value of administrative materials is based on the utility in the conduct of current or future administrative affairs.

Appraisal: (1) Archival appraisal is the process of evaluating documents to determine whether they are to be archived indefinitely, retained for a shorter period, or disposed of in some other way (e.g. sold, donated, destroyed). (2) The monetary valuation of a gift, usually determined at the request of a library, museum, or archives by a professional appraiser familiar with the market for the type of item. Knowing the value of an item may be necessary in case of theft, for insurance purposes, or in deciding whether the expense of restoration is justified. Appraisal can be an expensive undertaking because the appraiser's specialised knowledge of books, bibliography, and reference sources must often be extensive.

Archival description: See *Description*

Archival collection: Refers to the accumulation of any type of materials (e.g. books, personal papers, manuscripts, photographs, electronic media, reports, records) by one or more persons, or by a corporate entity, donated or housed in an archive. See also *Fonds* and *Holdings*.

Archival outreach: See *Outreach*.

Archival value: The decision, following appraisal by a knowledgeable expert (or experts), that a document, record, or group of records is worth preserving, permanently or for an indefinite period.

Archive: (*Noun*) The building, facility, or area that houses an archival collection. See also *Repository*. (*Verb*) To place documents in storage, usually to preserve them as a historical, informational, legal, or evidential record, permanently or for a finite or indefinite period of time.

Archives: (1) An organised collection of the non-current records of the activities of a business, government, organisation, institution, or other corporate body, or the personal papers of one or more individuals, families, or groups. (2) The office or organisation responsible for appraising, selecting, preserving, and providing access to archival materials. Archives can be classified in three broad categories: government archives (e.g. National Archives and Records Administration), in-house archives maintained by a parent institution, and collecting archives (e.g. manuscript libraries, film archives, genealogical archives, sound archives, personal archives). Compare with *Archive*.

Archives policy: A formal written statement defining the authority under which an archival programme operates, the scope of its activities (e.g. mission, objectives, conditions/restrictions), and the range of services it provides.

Archivist: The person responsible for managing and maintaining an archival collection, usually a librarian with special training in archival practices and methods. Archivists can also have obtained their training through a history or public history department or through a certification programme. Archivist's duties include the identification and appraisal of records of archival value, authentication, accessioning, description and documentation, facilitation of access and use, preservation and conservation, and exhibition and publication to benefit scholarship and satisfy public interest.

Arrangement: The process of putting archives and records into order following accepted archival principles, especially those of provenance and original order. If, after detailed examination, the original order is found to be completely random, the archivist may, after careful documenting of the original order, substitute an impartial arrangement that facilitates use.

Collection file: File created for each material donated to the archives. The file should keep information regarding the names of persons and/or organisations who have donated to archives. A well-maintained collection file should document any restrictions on preservation, use, or disposition of donated items, and provide current contact information. In case of deaccessioning a collection, it is wise to check discards against such a file to ascertain if a prior agreement was made with the donor concerning final disposition. See also *Donor file*.

Conservation: The use of physical or chemical methods to ensure the survival of manuscripts, books, and other documents, for example, the storage of materials under controlled environmental conditions or the treatment of mildew-infected paper with a chemical inhibitor. Non-invasive techniques are preferred as a means of preserving items in their original condition. In a more general sense, any measures taken to protect archival matter from damage or deterioration, including initial examination, documentation, treatment, and preventive care supported by research. Compare with *Preservation*.

Copyright: The exclusive legal rights granted by a government to an author, editor, compiler, composer, playwright, publisher, or distributor to publish, produce, sell, or distribute copies of a literary, musical, dramatic, artistic, or other work, within certain limitations (fair use and first sale). Such rights may be transferred or sold to others and do not necessarily pass with ownership of the work itself.

Creator: The person or organisation that created, received, and accumulated materials in a collection. A creator may also be a donor but not all donors are creators.

Custody: The action taken by an archive of physically obtaining possession of a collection.

Deaccession: In archives, the process of removing records or documents from official custody, undertaken after careful consideration, usually as the result of a decision to transfer the material to another custodian or because the legal owner desires its return or the material is found upon reappraisal to be of doubtful authenticity or inappropriate for the collection.

Deaccessioning action plan: A deaccessioning action plan sets the procedures, instructions, and chain of command to remove (deaccession) a collection from the archive.

Deed of gift: The legal agreement between the archives and donor documenting the term of a donation. See also *Donor agreement.*

Description: The process of recording information about the nature and content of the records in archival custody. The description identifies such features as provenance, arrangement, format and contents, and presents them in a standardised form.

Donation: In archives, a voluntary deposit of records by a person or organisation in which both legal title and physical custody are formally transferred by the donor to the institution maintaining the archives. In libraries, the term is used synonymously with gift. See also *Collection file.*

Donor: A person or organisation that has donated materials to an archive. Donors may be also the creators of the material donated but not all creators are donors. See also *Creator.*

Donor agreement: A formal written agreement between the person or organisation donating archival materials to a library, archives, or other institution and the recipient, which (1) describes the materials, (2) specifies the nature of the transaction (gift, deposit, loan, purchase, or a combination of these), (3) states the responsibilities of the depository for the physical maintenance and accessibility of the materials, and (4) clarifies any rights in and restrictions on use of the materials by the depository, its patrons, or the donor, including copyright. A copy of the donor agreement is retained by the recipient in the donor file for purposes of documentation and reference. See also *Deed of gift.*

Donor file: A file consisting of all related documentation generated while obtaining an archival collection for the archive. See also *Collection file.*

Donor register: A log with brief descriptions of collections accepted into the archives. The log should include donors' contact information and any relevant data regarding their donation.

Electronic record: See *Record*

Encoded archival description (EAD): EAD is a non-proprietary standard, a subset of a broader encoding standard called SGML (Standard Generalised Mark-Up Language) of which HTML (Hypertext Mark-up Language) is also a subset. It was created to encode finding aid documents for access through the Internet. EAD was developed in 1993 on the initiative of the UC Berkeley Library and is maintained by the Library of Congress, in partnership with the Society of American Archivists.

Ephemera: Materials (physical or electronic) that, regardless of appearance, quality or quantity, at some point were considered disposable and of little value or no value and, through time, have become valuable in such a way that it has broadened their appeal and made them desirable to be collected and preserved by individuals, collectors, and archives. These materials become the non-traditional, alternative evidence of mainstream and non-mainstream groups in society.

Equality of access: An archival principle that ensures that archives provide access to their collections to all users without favouring one user over another.

Evidential value: This value of the materials is based on their capacity to furnish proof of facts concerning their creator or the events/activities to which they pertain.

Exhibition: The use of original archival materials or copies in a display to present ideas which inform or educate the viewer and/or promote the archives.

Finding aid: A published or unpublished guide, inventory, list, or other system for retrieving archival primary source materials that provides more detailed description of each item than is customary in a library catalogue record. Finding aids also exist in non-print formats (e.g. ASCII, HTML). In partnership with the Society of American Archivists, the Library of Congress maintains a standard called Encoded Archival Description (EAD) for encoding archival finding aids.

Fonds: The whole of the documents, regardless of form or medium, organically created and/or accumulated and used by a particular person, family, or corporate body in the course of that creator's activities and functions. See also *Archival collection*.

Gift: One or more books or other items donated to a library, usually by an individual but sometimes by a group, organisation, estate, or other library. In academic libraries, desk copies and review copies are sometimes received as gifts from members of the teaching faculty.

Most gifts of materials are unsolicited and arrive unexpectedly, but gift collections may also be solicited by the library. Donated items are usually evaluated in accordance with the library's collection development policy and either added to the collection or disposed of, usually in a book sale or exchange with another library. See also *Donation*.

Goal: (1) A projected desired outcome. Goals are usually expressed in abstract terms, with no time limit for realisation. The specifics by which they are to be attained are also left open. (2) In strategic planning, goals are the general directions or aims that an organisation commits to attaining in order to further its mission.

Holdings: The whole of the records and archival materials in the custody of an archival programme. See also *Archival collections*.

Informational value: This value of the materials is based on their usefulness for reference and research.

Intellectual control: The control established over the informational content of records and archives resulting from ascertaining and documenting their provenance, and from the processes of arrangement and description.

Intrinsic value: Value of the materials based on the inherent worth based on content, cultural significance, antiquity, past uses, etc.

Inventory: A list describing in varying degrees of detail the content of one or more elements of intellectual control of an archive. Inventories can be done at three different levels: box, file and item.

Linear foot: The standard record storage box (banker's box) = one cubic foot = two 0.5 linear feet document boxes.

Machine-readable records: In archives, records created and maintained in a medium that requires some kind of machine to access its content (e.g. microforms, sound recordings, video recordings, magnetic tape and disks, optical disks). For example, EAD records, MARC records. Compare with *Electronic records*.

Manuscript: (1) From the Latin phrase codex *manu scriptus*. Strictly speaking, a work of any kind (e.g. text, inscription, music score, map) written entirely by hand. A medieval manuscript is one written in Europe prior to the invention of printing from movable type (c. 1450). (2) Also refers to the handwritten or typescript copy of an author's work as submitted for publication, before printing.

Mission: The basic purpose or role of an organisation expressed succinctly in abstract terms. A clearly written mission statement is the basis for formulating achievable goals and objectives in strategic planning and serves as a constant reminder of the organisation's primary reason for existing.

Monetary value: This value of the materials refers to its worth in the marketplace, based on the appraisal performed by a person experienced in making such judgments.

Objective: A specific achievable outcome of actions taken to achieve a stated goal, usually expressed in measurable terms and subject to a time limit. Although an objective does not address the specific means by which the outcome is to be achieved, it should be based upon a realistic assessment of available resources. A good set of achievable objectives can serve as an inspiration and guide for an organisation in planning for the future, allocating resources, evaluating progress, adjusting strategy, and persevering until the desired result is achieved.

Original order: In archives, the principle that establishes that records should remain in the sequence in which they were maintained when in active use, unless the method of accumulation is determined upon inspection to have been so unsystematic as to render retrieval difficult, if not impossible. Existing relationships are preserved when documents remain as originally arranged, making it easier to prepare finding aids. Original order also has evidential value.

Outreach: To provide services and activities that inform and involve your stakeholders (e.g. donors, local communities, public in general) about the archival holdings and services of the archives.

Questionnaire: A list of written questions carefully formulated to be administered to a selected group of people for the purpose of gathering information (feedback) in a survey research. In libraries, patrons may be asked to fill out questionnaires designed to assess the perceived quality and usefulness of services and resources. The results are then compiled and analysed for use in planning.

Parent institution: Refers to an organisation's top level of management; the level to which most archivists and related staff work for and/or report to.

Preservation: Prolonging the existence of archival materials by maintaining them in a condition suitable for use, either in their original format or in a form more durable, through retention under proper environmental conditions or actions taken after a collection has been damaged to prevent further deterioration. Compare with *Conservation*.

Provenance: In archives, the succession of custodians responsible for creating, receiving, or accumulating a collection of records or personal papers. Authentication of archival materials requires that provenance be determined with certainty. The related principle of *respect des fonds* requires that records known to have originated from a given source be documented and retained separately from those of other agencies or persons, and in their original order and organisational context, whenever possible.

Reading room: A room or area set aside for supervised consultation of archival materials by authorised users. Also known as search room and research room.

Record: Documents containing data or information of any kind and in any form, created or received and accumulated by an organisation or person.

Reference: The range of activities involved in providing information from or about records and archives, e.g. making records and archives available for access and providing copies or reproductions of records and archives. See also *Reference services*.

Reference services: The facilities and services that enable the user to use the archives and its records once access to them is approved. See also *Reference*.

Repository: The building or room, or part thereof, set aside for the storage of archives and or collections. See also *Archive*.

Research room: See *Reading room*

Respect des fonds: The principle of provenance first developed by French archivists in the early nineteenth century under which the organic nature of the archival records of an individual or agency dictates that they be maintained separately with respect to source and in their original physical order, rather than combined or intermingled with those of different origin.

Search room: See *Reading room*

Selection: The process of deciding which materials should be added to an archival collection. Selection decisions are usually made on the basis of reviews and standard collection development tools by people designated as the selectors in specific subject areas, usually based on their interests and fields of specialisation. See also *Appraisal*.

Special collections: Some libraries segregate from the general collections rare books, manuscripts, papers, and other items that are (1) of a certain form, (2) on certain subjects, (3) of a certain time period or geographical area, (4) in fragile or poor condition, or (5) especially valuable. Such materials are usually not allowed to circulate and access to them may be restricted. There may be archival collections as part of the materials managed and stored by this entity.

Stakeholders: In the context of this book, stakeholders refers to the individuals or groups concerned with their institutions' archives (e.g. donors, administrators, local community groups, general public).

Strategic plan: The final document produced after having gone through a strategic planning process. It is easier to develop a strategic plan once the mission and vision of the organisation have been completed. See also *Strategic planning*.

Strategic planning: Long-term future planning or the systematic process by which a company, organisation, or institution (or one of its units) formulates achievable policy objectives for future growth and development over a period of years, ranging from one to five years, or even more. The strategic plan is based on the organisation's mission and goals and on a realistic assessment of the resources, human and material, available to implement the plan.

Survey: A method of collecting information directly from people about ideas, feelings, etc. A survey can be a self-administered questionnaire that someone fills out alone or with assistance. A survey can also be an interview that is done in person or on the phone (Fink and Kosecoff, 1998: 1). See also *User survey*.

Transfer: The process of changing the physical custody of archives. This is a separate action from transferring the legal title of the materials. See also *Donation* and *Deed of gift*.

User(s): Person(s) who consults archival materials held at an archive, usually in a search room. Also referred to as *researchers*.

User survey: A questionnaire administered to users of a library or library system to find out what brings them to the library, how they normally use the resources and services it provides, their subject evaluation of the quality of their library experiences, and any suggestions for improvement (feedback).

Vision: (1) A statement describing an organisation's state and function. (2) A motivational statement that challenges and inspires an organisation to achieve its mission (McNamara, 1999).

Further reading

Chapter 1

History of archives

Brosius, M. (2004) *Archives and Archival Traditions: Concepts of Recordkeeping in the Ancient World.* Oxford: Oxford University Press.

Posner, E. M. and O'Toole, J. M. (2003) *Archives in the Ancient World.* Society of American Archivists, Archival Classics Series. Cambridge, MA: Harvard University Press.

Steedman, C. (2002) *Dust: The Archive and Cultural History.* New Brunswick, NJ: Rutgers University Press.

Introducing archives

Cook, T. and Dodds, G. (eds) (2003) *Imagining Archives: Essays and Reflections by Hugh A. Taylor.* Lanham, MD: Scarecrow Press.

Daniels, M. and Walch, T. (eds) (1984) *Modern Archives Reader: Basic Readings on Archival Theory and Practice.* Washington DC: National Archives Trust Fund Board.

Ellis, R. and Walne, P. (eds) (2003) *Selected Writings of Sir Hilary Jenkinson.* Chicago, IL: Society of American Archivists, Archival Classics Series.

Schellenberg, T. R. (2003) *Modern Archives Principles and Techniques*. Chicago, IL: Society of American Archivists, Archival Classics Series.

Williams, C. (2002) *Archives in the UK and the Government Agenda*. Liverpool: Liverpool University Centre for Archives Studies.

Establishing archives

Archives Association of British Columbia (1999) *A Manual for Small Archives*. Vancouver: Archives Association of British Columbia. Partially Revised 1994 ©1999; Available at: *http://aabc.bc.ca/aabc/msa/default.htm*.

Ellis, J. (ed.) (1999) *Keeping Archives*, 2nd edn. Port Melbourne, Victoria: Thorpe in association with The Australian Society of Archivists.

Hunter, Gregory S. (2030) *Developing and Maintaining Practical Archives: A How to Do it Manual*, 2nd edn. New York: Neal-Schuman Publishers, Inc.

Maher, W. J. (1992) *The Management of College and University Archives*. Chicago, IL: The Society of American Archivists and Scarecrow Press, Inc.

Chapter 2

Surveys

Creswell, J. W. (2002) *Research Design: Qualitative, Quantitative, and Mixed Methods Approaches*, 2nd edn. Thousand Oaks, CA: SAGE Publications.

Fink, A. and Kosecoff, J. 1998 *How to Conduct Surveys: A Step-by-Step Guide*, 2nd edn. Thousand Oaks, CA: Sage Publications.

Needs assessment

Gupta, K. (1998) *A Practical Guide to Needs Assessment.* San Francisco, CA: Jossey-Bass/Pfeiffer.

Soriano, F. (1995) *Conducting Needs Assessments: A Multidisciplinary Approach.* Thousand Oaks, CA: Sage Publications.

Strategic planning

Matthews, J. (2005) *Strategic Planning and Management for Library Managers.* Westport, CT: Libraries Unlimited.

Wallace, L. K. (2004) *Libraries, Mission & Marketing: Writing Mission Statements that Work.* Chicago, IL: American Library Association.

Budget

Dropkin, M. and LaTouche, B. (1998) *The Budget-Building Book for Nonprofits: A Step-by-Step Guide for Managers and Boards.* San Francisco, CA: Jossey-Bass, Nonprofit & Public Management Series.

Farmer, L. S. J. (1993) *When Your Library Budget Is Almost Zero.* Westport, CT: Libraries Unlimited.

Hallam, A. W. and Dalston, T. R. (2005) *Managing Budgets and Finances: A How-to-Do-It Manual for Librarians and Information Professionals.* How to Do It Manuals for Librarians, No. 138. New York, NY: Neal-Schuman Publishers.

Fundraising

Brewer, E. W., Achilles, C. M., Fuhriman, J. R. and Hollingsworth, C. (2001) *Finding Funding: Grantwriting from Start to Finish, Including Project Management and Internet Use*. Thousand Oaks, CA: Sage Publications.

Keegan, P. B. (1994) *Fund-raising for Nonprofits: How to Build a Community Partnership*. Reprint edn. New York, NY: Harper Collins.

Swan, J. (2002) *Fund-raising for Libraries: 25 Proven Ways to Get More Money for Your Library*. How-To-Do-It Manuals for Libraries. New York, NY: Neal-Schuman Publishers.

Chapter 4

Appraisal and tools

Craig, B. L. (2004) *Archival Appraisal: Theory and Practice*. Munich: KG Saur.

Fleckner, J. A. (1977) *Archives & Manuscripts: Surveys*. Chicago, IL: Society of American Archivists.

Electronic records (appraisal and management)

Dearstyne, B. W. (2001) *Effective Approaches for Managing Electronic Records and Archives*. Lanham, MD: Scarecrow Press, Inc.

Chapter 5

Donor relations, advocacy

Freeman Finch, E. T. (1994) *Advocating Archives: An Introduction to Public Relations for Archivists*. Chicago,

IL and Lanham, MD: Society of American Archivists and Scarecrow Press, Inc.

Legal and ethical issues

Benedict, K. M. (2003) *Ethics and the Archival Profession: Introduction and Case Studies*. Chicago, IL: Society of American Archivists.

Lipinski, T. A. (ed.) (2002) *Libraries, Museums, and Archives: Legal Issues and Ethical Challenges in the New Information Age*. Lanham, MD: Scarecrow Press, Inc.

MacNeil, H. (1992) *Without Consent: The Ethics of Disclosing Personal Information in Public Archives*. Chicago, IL and Lanham, MD: Society of American Archivists and Scarecrow Press, Inc.

Chapter 6

Preservation

Cunha, G. (1988) *Methods of Evaluation to Determine The Preservation Needs in Libraries and Archives: A RAMP Study*. Paris: [Prepared for the] General Information Programme and UNISIST, UNESCO. Out of print. Available at: *http://www.unesco.org/webworld/ramp/html/r8816e/r8816e00.htm*.

Dollar, C. (1999) *Authentic Electronic Records: Strategies for Long-Term Access*. Chicago, IL: Cohasset Associates, Inc.

Harvey, R. (1993) *Preservation in Libraries: A Reader*. London; New York: Bowker-Saur.

Merrill, Andrea T. (ed.) (2003) *The Strategic Stewardship of Cultural Resources: To Preserve and Protect.* Binghamton, NY: Haworth Press.

Ritzenthaler, M. L. (1993) *Preserving Archives and Manuscripts.* Chicago, IL: Society of American Archivists.

Wilhelm, H. (1993) *Permanence and Care of Color Photographs: Traditional and Digital Color Prints, Color Negatives, Slides, and Motion Pictures.* Grinnell, IA: Preservation Publishing Company.

Chapter 7

Arrangement and description

Carmichael, D. W. (2004) *Organizing Archival Records: A Practical Method of Arrangement and Description for Small Archives*, 2nd edn. Walnut Creek, CA: AltaMira Press.

International Council of Archives (ICA) (1999) *ISAD (G): General International Standard Archival Description*, 2nd edn. Paris: Adopted by the Committee on Descriptive Standards, Stockholm, Sweden, 19–22 September. Available at the International Council of Archives website at *http://www.ica.org/biblio/cds/isad_g_2e.pdf.*

Roe, K. D. (2005) *Arranging and Describing Archives and Manuscripts* (Archival Fundamentals Series II). Chicago, IL: Society of American Archivists.

Encoded archival description

Dooley, J. (ed.) (1998) *Encoded Archival Description: Context, Theory and Case Studies.* Chicago, IL: Society of American Archivists.

Dow, E. H. (2005) *Creating EAD-Compatible Finding Guides on Paper*. Lanham, MD: Scarecrow Press, Inc.

Encoded Archival Description Working Group of the Society of American Archivists and the Network Development and MARC Standards Office of the Library of Congress. (2003) *Encoded Archival Description: Tag Library* (Version 2002). Chicago, IL: Society of American Archivists.

Chapter 8

Reference services

Pugh, M. J. (2005) *Providing Reference Services for Archives and Manuscripts* (Archival Fundamentals Series II). Chicago, IL: Society of American Archivists.

Citing sources

The University of Chicago Press Staff (ed.) (2003) 15th edn *The Chicago Manual of Style*. Chicago, IL: The University of Chicago Press.

Gibaldi, J. (ed.) (2003) *MLA Handbook for Writers of Research Papers*, 6th edn. New York, NY: The Modern Language Association of America.

Turabian, K. L. (1996) *A Manual for Writers of Term Papers, Theses, and Dissertations*, 6th edn. Chicago, IL: The University of Chicago Press.

Security

O'Neill, R. K. (1998) *Management of Library and Archival Security: From the Outside Looking In*. Binghamton, NY: Haworth Press.

Traditional exhibits

Brown, M. E. and Power, R. (2005) *Exhibits in Libraries: A Practical Guide.* Jefferson, NC: McFarland & Company.

Serrell, B. (1996) *Exhibit Labels: An Interpretive Approach.* Walnut Creek, CA: Altamira Press.

Lord, B. (2001) *The Manual of Museum Exhibitions.* Walnut Creek, CA: Altamira Press.

Digital/virtual collections

Grout, C., Purdy, P. and Rymer, J. (2000) *Creating Digital Resources for the Visual Arts: Standards and Good Practice.* Oxford: Oxbow Books.

Hughes, L. (2004) *Digitizing Collections: Strategic Issues for the Information Manager.* London: FACET, the imprint of the Chartered Institute of Library and Information Professionals (formerly the British Library Association).

Kalfatovic, M. R. (2002) *Creating a Winning Online Exhibition: A Guide for Libraries, Archives, and Museums.* Chicago, IL: American Library Association.

Stielow, F. J. (2003) *Building Digital Archives, Descriptions, and Displays: A How-To-Do-It Manual for Librarians and Archivists.* New York, NY: Neal-Schuman Publishers, Inc.

Outreach in general

Arant, W. and Mosley, A. P. (eds) (2000) *Library Outreach, Partnerships, and Distance Education: Reference Librarians at the Gateway.* Binghamton, NY: Haworth Press.

Bibliography

Alliance for Nonprofit Management (year unknown) 'What's in a vision statement?'; available at: *http://www .allianceonline.org/FAQ/strategic_planning/what_s_in_ vision_statement.faq* (accessed: 22 December 2005).

Ellis, J. (ed.) (1999) *Keeping Archives.* 2nd edn. Port Melbourne, Victoria: Thorpe in association with The Australian Society of Archivists.

Fink, A. and Kosecoff, J. (1998) *How to Conduct Surveys: A Step-by-Step Guide.* 2nd edn. Thousand Oaks, CA: Sage Publications.

Maher, W. J. (1992) *The Management of College and University Archives.* Metuchen, NJ: The Society of American Archivists and The Scarecrow Press, Inc.

McKemmish, S. (1999) 'Introducing archives and archival programs' in Ellis, Judith (ed.) *Keeping Archives.* 2nd edn. Port Melbourne, Victoria: Thorpe in association with The Australian Society of Archivists; pp. 1–24.

McNamara, C. (1999) 'Basics of developing mission, vision and values statements'; available at: *http://www .managementhelp.org/plan_dec/str_plan/stmnts.htm* (accessed: 22 December 2005).

Reitz, J. M. (2004) *Dictionary for Library and Information Science.* Westport, CT: Libraries Unlimited.

Schellenberg, T. R. (1956) 'The appraisal of modern records', *Bulletins of the National Archives*, Number 8 (October). Also available at the National Archives and Records Administration (NARA), USA website, at:

http://www.archives.gov/research/alic/reference/archives-resources/appraisal-of-records.html (accessed: 22 December 2005).

Schwirtlich A.-M. and Reed, B. (1999) 'Managing the acquisition process' in *Keeping Archives*, 2nd edn. Port Melbourne, Victoria: Thorpe in association with The Australian Society of Archivists; pp. 137–56.

Swinton, L. (year unknown) 'How to do a SWOT analysis: strategic planning made easy'; available at: *http://www.trans4mind.com/counterpoint/swinton3.shtml* (accessed: 12 December 2005).

The Coaching Lounge (year unknown) 'Strategic planning: Can strategic planning help your business?'; available at: *http://thecoachinglounge.com/strategicplanning.html* (accessed: 12 December 2005).

Tashakkori, A. and Teddlie, C. (eds) (2003) *Handbook of Mixed Methods in Social & Behavioral Research*. Thousand Oaks, CA: Sage Publications.

Turabian, K. L. (1996) *A Manual for Writers of Term Papers, Theses, and Dissertations*. 6th edn. Chicago, IL: The University of Chicago Press.

University of Chicago Press Staff (eds) *The Chicago Manual of Style* (2003) 15th edn. Chicago, IL: The University of Chicago Press.

Vogt, W. P. (1993) *Dictionary of Statistics and Methodology: a Nontechnical Guide for the Social Sciences*. Thousand Oaks, CA: Sage Publications.

Index